BLACK SKINS, FRENCH VOICES

Caribbean Ethnicity and Activism in Urban France

DAVID BERISS

University of New Orleans

A Member of the Perseus Books Group

Photographs courtesy of author except where otherwise indicated.

All maps by Samara Ebinger.

Copyright © 2004 by David Beriss

Westview Press books are available at special discounts for bulk purchases in the
United States by corporations, institutions, and other organizations. For more
information, please contact the Special Markets Department at the Perseus Books
Group, 11 Cambridge Center, Cambridge MA 02142, or call (800) 255-1514 or
(617) 252-5298, or e-mail special.markets@perseusbooks.com.

Published in the United States of America by Westview Press, 5500 Central Avenue,
Boulder, Colorado 80301–2877 and in the United Kingdom by Westview Press, 12
Hid's Copse Road, Cumnor Hill,Oxford OX2 9JJ.

Find us on the World Wide Web at www.westviewpress.com

Cataloging-in-Publication data is available from the Library of Congress.
ISBN-10 0–8133–4254–6 (pb) ISBN-13 978–0–8133–4254–2 (pb)

Contents

Series Editor Preface   *vii*

Acknowledgments   *xi*

Introduction   *xiii*

1   FINDING CREOLE IDENTITIES
     IN MARTINIQUE AND PARIS   1

2   WHAT IS THE PRICE OF FRENCHNESS?   25

3   BETRAYED ANTILLES, BROKEN FRENCH PROMISES   51

4   *BOUDIN, RHUM,* AND *ZOUK*: PERFORMANCE AND
     CULTURAL CONFRONTATION   73

5   CAN MAGIC FIX A BROKEN CULTURE?   89

6   IN THIS WORLD, BUT NOT OF IT   105

7   CONCLUSION: CREOLIZING FRANCE   123

Glossary   *135*

References   *139*

Index   *149*

Series Editor Preface

France is a country of contradictions. It has been the most stalwart proponent of European integration while positioning itself on the front line in a battle against U.S.–led cultural globalization. The country has long served as an archetype of the modern European nation-state—politically unified and seemingly homogeneous culturally—while being divided by profound regional differences and separatist movements (such as in Corsica).

Where a distant gaze may clearly see cultural homogeneity, closer inspection reveals great diversity. The France that David Beriss describes in this book is an amalgamation of many countries, and his nuanced description leads the reader to see the folly in discussing France in the singular. In cosmopolitan Paris we glimpse the self-proclaimed guardians of French high culture, in a working-class suburb we encounter the subtle xenophobia of local politics, and everywhere we see the immigrant populations from North Africa, southern Europe, and the French Antilles. It is a place of de jure uniformity ("Frenchness") but de facto plurality. It is in this ambiguous space that Beriss sets his narrative.

There is a long-standing French tradition of romanticizing the exotic (Paul Gauguin's images of Tahitian women come to mind), but this allure is tempered by a fear of cultural dilution and pollution. Mainstream French appreciation of foreign music, for example, stops short of embracing these traditions as part of a national patrimony. In *Black Skins, French Voices* we see this tension from the viewpoint of the immigrant Antillean community. Beriss begins his narrative in the French Antilles, on the Caribbean islands of

Martinique and Guadeloupe, where he too gets caught up in the flow of people to France. Today about one-third of all Antilleans live in France, almost as many as live on either Martinique or Guadeloupe. As residents of a French overseas territory, Antillean immigrants are French citizens. One might think that this would ease the trauma of migration, but accompanying their citizenship is an implicit expectation of cultural assimilation: if you are French, you should act French.

Most mainstream French politicians have adopted public discourses of multiculturalism in acknowledgment of the country's diversifying population. Yet the anti-immigrant far right has also seen a dramatic surge in support in recent years. And French social policies continue to promote cultural assimilation. As I pen these lines, the French National Assembly is debating a bill to ban conspicuous religious attire (the target being Muslim head wear) in public schools. Paradoxically, this is intended to promote the stalwart liberal cause of secular education while undermining the *au courant* liberal concern with multicultural inclusion.

Beriss argues that French domestic public policy is primarily oriented toward issues of class while Antillean activists call for reforms that address ethnic divisions in their own right. To these immigrant populations, elements of Antillean culture take on fetishized symbolic roles. Eating *boudin* sausages, drinking rum, dancing to *zouk* music—such iconic yet quotidian aspects of Antillean life acquire new political meanings in the context of French cultural politics. Yet these are not uncontested, and Beriss shows how some activists lament the minstrelization of Antillean culture.

Black Skins, French Voices makes an important contribution to the ethnography of nation building in a globalized world. Beriss takes us behind the scenes of French cultural politics, showing the little battles that are fought daily as part of a larger, largely uncoordinated campaign. We see, for example, the contested meanings of the bicentennial Bastille Day celebrations of 1989 and the World Cup soccer championship in 1998. We are made privy to debates over what is *le culturel* among Antillean theater troupes in Paris. In representing the diversity of French society Beriss does not gloss over the complexities of cultural hybridization—seen, for example, in the link between French spiritualism and Antillean magic.

This book also makes an important contribution to the field of anthropology as a whole—particularly on issues of race and class, immigration, and national identity. Looking at residents of the Caribbean islands of Martinique and Guadeloupe, both at home and as immigrants in Paris, Beriss takes an approach that is at once intensely global and intimately local. He shows how they manage their identities as both French and Caribbean in the heated context of French cultural politics, as well as the changes that immigration is making in Western European societies.

The writing is accessible, and the narrative engages readers in the story line. At the same time Beriss does not shy away from pressing issues of topical concern in the discipline as a whole. In this regard, the book fits neatly with the aims of the *Westview Case Studies in Anthropology* series, which presents works that recognize the peoples under study as active agents enmeshed in global as well as local systems of politics, economics, and cultural flows. Beriss accomplishes this through his fascinating study of transnational cultural formation.

In presenting rich humanistic and social scientific data borne of the dialectic engagement of fieldwork, this volume, along with the other books in the series, moves toward realizing the full pedagogical potential of anthropology: imparting to the reader an empathetic understanding of alternative ways of viewing and acting in the world as well as a solid basis for critical thought regarding the historically contingent nature of our own cultural knowledge.

Edward F. Fischer
Nashville, Tennessee

Acknowledgments

This book has been a long time in the making, and acknowledging all the contributions made by others over the many years since I began this research would be impossible. I must first thank Martha Ward, without whose encouragement, guidance, sharp editing skills, and insights into the world of publishing this book might never have been completed. She put more effort into this project than anyone except me. Jeffrey Ehrenreich contributed moral and material support far beyond what I might reasonably have expected of a colleague, as well as constant insights into the value of editorial experience. Martha, Jeffrey, and my other colleagues in the Department of Anthropology at the University of New Orleans, including J. Richard Shenkel, Richard Beavers, Malcolm Webb, and Ann Edwards, provided encouragement and intellectual support while I finished this book, and I am grateful for their patience.

The initial research and writing for this project was inspired by Susan Carol Rogers at New York University. It was Susan who convinced me to become an anthropologist in the first place, and I have never regretted that decision. Constance Sutton, also at NYU, helped me frame this project and understand the Caribbean. I am sure she will be pleased that it has finally been published. Professors Owen Lynch, Tony Judt, and Karen Blu all provided helpful insights and commentary on early stages of the project. My thinking about ethnicity, France, Europe, and the Caribbean has been shaped in conversations over the years with Richard Price, Sally Price, Catherine Benoit, Katherine Browne, Ellen Schnepel, David A. B. Murray, Susan Hyatt,

Caroline Brettell, Jeffrey Cole, Lawrence Taylor, Tom Wilson, and many others too numerous to mention. Ted Fischer, Karl Yambert, and Iris Richmond have provided valuable editorial insights. Samara Ebinger, a graduate assistant in the Department of Geography, University of New Orleans, created all the maps. I am grateful to them all.

None of what follows would have been possible without the help of many people in both France and the Antilles. Some of the people who were especially helpful with my research in Martinique include Jean-Paul Césaire, Lambert Félix-Prudent, Christian Bertin, Joël Caserus, Christian March, Daniel Schlupp, Alex Legendri, Isabelle Gratiant, Fabienne Florimond, and Edgar Menil. The discretion of ethnographic research requires that the many others who answered my questions remain anonymous.

Likewise, most of the Antilleans and metropolitan French people with whom I worked in Paris remain anonymous in the following chapters. However, none of this would have been possible without their cooperation and active guidance. Of the people I can mention, I would like especially to thank Father Pierre Lacroix, Pierre Pastel, Jean Galap, Julie Lirus-Galap, Christian Renoir, Dominique Jacques-Philippe, Daniel Boukman, and Michel Giraud.

The research for this book was supported by a variety of sources, including the National Science Foundation, the Institute for Intercultural Studies, a Bourse Chateaubriand from the French government, and a faculty research and travel grant from the University of New Orleans. I am grateful to all of these organizations for supporting my work.

Finally, this book would never have been possible without the insights, advice (which I nearly always followed), encouragement, and moral and material support of Jeanne Kessler. Jeanne was part of the project from the very beginning, when she accompanied me on my first research trip to Martinique. Over the years and across a variety of continents, many of my ideas and much of my capacity to work can be attributed to Jeanne. I am, above all, grateful for her patience.

Although they may not know it yet, Zoe Beriss and Nina Beriss helped brighten my perspective and raised my spirits in moments of exhaustion and despair. Someday they will write their own books.

While I have benefited deeply from the help of everyone I have mentioned here, and from many others, all errors and omissions are, of course, my own.

Introduction

This book is about the choices black French citizens make when they move from Martinique and Guadeloupe to Paris and discover that they are not fully French. It shows how ethnic activists in the Afro-Caribbean diaspora organize to demand what has never been available to them in France—the right to be full citizens and at the same time maintain their distinct culture and history. About 337,000 people of French Antillean origin live in metropolitan France today. Unlike immigrants from North Africa, Turkey, or sub-Saharan Africa, Antilleans are French citizens with deep roots in French history. Indeed, the Caribbean islands they come from have been part of France for more than three centuries. Recruited by the French government to work in public sector jobs that are not open to noncitizens, Antilleans were for many years an invisible population, dispersed throughout the Paris region, with few community organizations and little political activism. As French citizens, Antilleans in theory have little need to organize as a community.

Beginning in the early 1980s, however, activists in the Antillean community began to recognize that their status as citizens did not protect them from the growth of racism in France. They began to form community organizations and work toward creating an effective public voice for Antilleans. From neighborhood groups interested in promoting traditional Martinican and Guadeloupan dance and music to politically charged associations, these new cultural activists denounced French colonialism, challenged racism, and demanded political representation. The assertion of immigrant cultures and consciousness—by Antilleans and other immigrant activists—challenged

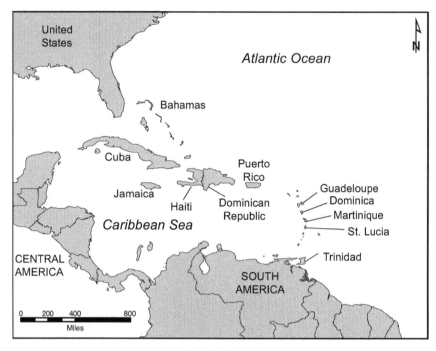

The Caribbean.

French integration policies and sparked national and international debate about the meaning of being French. *Black Skins, French Voices* is situated at the intersection of changing French ideas and policies regarding ethnic diversity and Antillean demands for recognition. It shows the creative, exciting struggles of Antilleans to remake French culture on their own terms.

FRENCHNESS DENIED, THE CARIBBEAN RECLAIMED

Black Skins, French Voices grows out of more than a decade of field research in France and the French Caribbean. In 1988 in Martinique, I began to interview cultural activists and artists and attended the festivals and art shows they organized for the city of Fort-de-France. I talked with union members, leaders of an association that promoted the teaching of Creole language and culture, and members of the city's Rotary Club. At lunch with the Rotarians, learning to spice my soup with fresh *piment,* or drinking rum-infused *shrub* in a Creole teacher's kitchen, I found that conversations always came back to confusion and anxiety about how to be Martinican in the shadow of France. I sought insight into how Antilleans organize their political lives. Later I real-

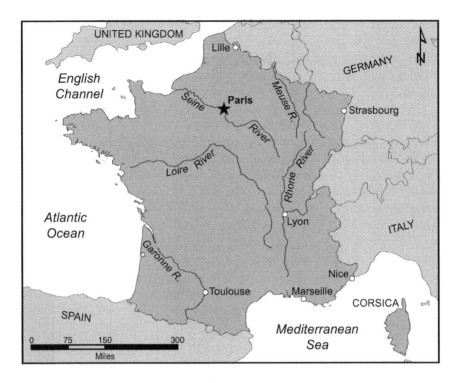

France.

ized that what drew these Martinicans together was a search for a common voice. Although their demands were diverse, affirming their existence as Martinicans in a postcolonial French context required that they find a way for that voice to be heard.

In Paris the following year, my first problem was to find Antilleans acting like Antilleans. Martinicans in Martinique are a majority, but in Paris they are a minority, dispersed in the anonymous apartment blocks of the city's working-class neighborhoods and suburbs. There is no neighborhood an anthropologist could call Antillean. The contours of the community are submerged in the urban fabric of Paris. Like many Antillean migrants, I first turned to the government agency charged with organizing the social "insertion" of migrants from the overseas departments. A Guadeloupan priest who ran a Catholic community center for Antilleans in France put me in touch with a wide variety of community leaders. I met with Antilleans in professional associations (e.g., subway workers and postal workers), social service providers, organizers of student groups, and members of musical, theater, and dance clubs. I interviewed religious leaders, government bureaucrats, social workers, artists, and intellectuals. Like Antilleans themselves, I began to pay close attention to the ways the French media represented them, scrutinizing television programs, movies, newspapers, and magazines for signs of Antillean culture and society. Caribbean Paris, linked by the rhythms of *zouk* music on independent radio stations, moved to the front of my attention.

Decades of struggle against colonialism in the French Antilles led Antilleans of color to believe that assimilation was the most promising route to liberation from the domination of white planters. Putting aside their own Caribbean cultures was the price the French demanded, and they were willing to pay. Once in metropolitan France, however, postcolonial Antilleans found themselves classified as non-French, a visible minority routinely exposed to racism. In this book, I show how Antillean militants confront the broken promise of individual equality with demands to be both fully French and fully Antillean. As they work to be equal citizens and equally recognized as culturally distinct, Antilleans use art, social policy, and religion to shape their identities in ways that are recognizably French in form but Caribbean in substance. The creative ways they draw on French and Caribbean terms and concepts to shape their communities define new ways for cultures to cross the Atlantic.

POSTMODERN ETHNICITY IN POSTCOLONIAL PARIS

The title of this book, *Black Skins, French Voices*, pays homage to a pathbreaking analysis of the psychology of race and racism, *Black Skin, White Masks*, written in 1952 by Frantz Fanon, a Martinican intellectual and psychiatrist. Fanon wrote his book amid growing struggles against colonialism in Africa, Asia, and the Caribbean—struggles he later joined, fighting for Algerian independence from France; he also wrote in the period immediately following the incorporation of the French Antilles into France, as *départements d'outre-mer* (overseas departments). He argued that the logic of racial and colonial relations made black people feel inferior, leading them to imitate white society, efforts that whites failed to recognize as having value. Although Fanon wrote in racial terms, his analysis was grounded in Martinique, and he noted that the experiences of black Americans or Africans would be different. He believed that racism would only be overcome when Martinicans demanded recognition from the French, not as perfect imitation French people but as something distinct, as Martinicans.

Much has changed since Fanon's book. In 1952, few Antilleans lived in metropolitan France. Fanon's analysis was as much about the confrontation between two societies, France and Martinique, locked in a nearly colonial relationship, as it was about relations between black and white people. Richard Price (1998) has examined the transformation of Martinican society since

Fanon's time, focusing on how Martinicans make French ideologies and practices their own. Today nearly as many Antilleans live in France as in either Martinique or Guadeloupe, amid millions of other immigrants from the Third World, many from France's former colonies. These immigrants are engaged in self-conscious processes of sorting out what it means to be Antillean (or North African, Muslim, Vietnamese, etc.) in postcolonial France. Their demands for recognition have also triggered debates in France about the meaning of being French. Ironically, it was just this sort of postmodern negotiation of French and Antillean identities that Fanon called for in his book. Today that negotiation is less about race than about the creolization of French society and the reconfiguration of the meaning of state and nation there.

In what follows, I place debates about ethnicity and race in contemporary France in both a national and an international context. Like other recent ethnographers, I highlight the way social activists challenge how we think about community and politics (Baumann 1996; Gregory 1998; Sanjek 1998). This is a case study of the creative ways postcolonial (yet still black) citizens make themselves visible in a society that has historically denied legitimacy to ethnic activism. My goal is to introduce readers to a multicultural, multiracial urban setting, while not losing sight of how Antillean activism fits in a broad historical, national, and international context.

This book is an ethnography, focused on the social relations that structure people's lives, as well as on the terms and concepts they use to make sense of their lives. Antilleans in France, like people everywhere, draw on movies, literature, and social science to think about ethnicity (Limon 1999). I have chosen to include popular culture in my analysis, examining the impact of television, advertising, movies, and spectacular public events (from the 1989 bicentennial of the French revolution to the 1998 Soccer World Cup in Paris) on the lives and strategies of Antilleans. In addition, the French Antilles have been home to some of the most significant literary and intellectual figures of twentieth-century anticolonial and postcolonial movements, including Aimé Césaire and, of course, Frantz Fanon. I show how their ideas and those of their intellectual descendants (from *négritude* to *créolité*) have been essential to the creation of Antillean culture in France.

Black Skins, French Voices is also an ethnography of transnational migration. In line with other recent ethnographies (Ong 1999; Schiller and Fouron 2001), I show the importance of ongoing relations with the Caribbean in the lives of Antilleans in France. Many studies of transnational migrations focus on immigration to the United States. With its focus on France and the French Caribbean, *Black Skins, French Voices* provides an important comparative case study. By showing how Antilleans think and act across borders, it adds a French perspective to the shaping of the "Black Atlantic," first analyzed by Paul Gilroy (1993).

READING *BLACK SKINS, FRENCH VOICES*

Along with its homage to Fanon, the title of this book refers to the central dilemma confronting Antilleans in France. They are French citizens, deeply familiar with French culture and society. Despite their apparent Frenchness, they are marked as a visible minority in France. Their activism requires building a creative relationship between the two poles of being black and French. The first three chapters in this volume put that tension into a historical context. In Chapter 1, I ask who Antilleans in Paris are and why they want to become cultural activists. As French citizens, they do not face the same structural and legal constraints as other immigrants in France. Putting together a cultural movement among Antilleans is a difficult challenge, one that begins with finding causes and symbols that can bring together a community. I start by looking at how the question of cultural identity is posed in Martinique. Next I provide snapshots of the lives and actions of particular activists in Paris, revealing the experiences that lead them to become advocates and develop distinct strategies to assert ethnic difference in a French context. Conducting field research with this sort of group presented challenges similar to those faced by Antillean militants. I also tell the story of my own research, from my initial search for the ideas and practices that brought Antilleans together in Martinique, Guadeloupe, and Paris in the early 1990s, to more recent conversations.

Chapter 2 is framed by two spectacular events—the 1989 bicentennial of the French Revolution and the 1998 Soccer World Cup victory by a multicultural French team—that provided platforms for the display of and debate about French national identity and the place of immigrants and minorities in it. I draw on these events and other recent representations of immigrant experiences in film and literature to explore the changing meaning of culture, race, and community in France. I examine the development of postwar French immigration policies, showing how they set the stage for ethnic activism. Assimilation has been promised to immigrants—at the price of abandoning public attachment to their cultures of origin. For some immigrants, however, color and colonial origin seem to transcend the promise of assimilation and make acceptance into the French nation impossible. This provides the essential context for Antillean mobilization in France.

Chapter 3 opens with an examination of contrasting Antillean and French responses to the 1998 commemoration of the 150th anniversary of the abolition of slavery in the French colonies. Debates about the role of France in the enslavement of Africans and as their eventual liberator encapsulate current controversies about the value and possibility of assimilation into French culture for Antilleans. As French citizens, Antilleans are cultural insiders, but as dark-skinned postcolonials, they are visibly marked as outsiders. The French revolutionary ideal of assimilation has held out to Martinicans and Guadeloupans of color the promise of equality since the nineteenth-century struggle to overcome the domination of white planters. Becoming truly French has been the dominant ideology in Antillean anticolonial movements. Antilleans draw on this history and the anticolonial and postcolonial work of writers such as Aimé Césaire, Frantz Fanon, Edouard Glissant, and Patrick Chamoiseau to denounce racism and colonialism and to frame their claims for cultural recognition. Political and cultural movements, from *négritude* to *créolité*, help activists make sense of changing development policies in the French Caribbean, including departmentalization and the progressive inclusion of the French Antilles in the European Union.

Chapters 4–6 focus on the variety of strategies Antilleans in Paris develop in their efforts to demand recognition. Chapter 4 focuses on two different Antillean groups who chose cultural performance to assert their cultural distinctiveness and challenge the failure of France's assimilationist ideals. One group, composed of working-class Guadeloupan immigrants, performs amateur theater in nightclubs and at parties. Their self-written plays, rooted in nostalgia for a lost Antillean authenticity, also reflect experiences of racism and rejection in France. Members of the second group were born in France, but their parents grew up in the Antilles. Middle class and often university educated, these Antilleans use music, art, and fashion to show how Antillean culture is the cutting edge of creolization in France. Their performances provide a sharp critique of French assimilation ideologies and practices. At the same time, they model how "Caribbeanness" in France confronts French culture itself.

Chapter 5 examines a group of Antillean social workers, psychologists, and social scientists who use their research to shape public policies toward Antilleans in France. In a country in which class differences have long been central to the formation of social policy, these activists struggle to make the case for culture. They assert that Antilleans in France often suffer from a kind of cultural breakdown that alienates them from their own values—as expressed in magic, religion, kinship, and sexuality—in favor of corrupting French values. Situating themselves between the French government and the Antillean population, they work to train social workers to recognize specific Antillean cultural needs in France. These activists draw on French ideas about the role of the engaged intellectual to critique the place of Antilleans in French society. Yet the success of their efforts to bring culture to the French policy process may be limited by the racialization of French social policy in the last decade.

The majority of Antilleans are Catholic and in their island homes they regularly attend their local church. However, in Paris their perception that French churches are "cold" leads many to abandon participation. Lay groups around the city, organized by the Antillean Catholic center in Paris, work to make the French Church more responsive to Antilleans by an explicit assertion of Creole practices in the Church. However, these activists are painfully aware that they will remain a minority within the Church in France. They also seek to relate their activism to social service providers. This contrasts sharply with the Seventh-Day Adventist Church, which in Paris is predominantly Antillean. Yet Adventists are steadfast in their insistent demand to be Adventists first, Antilleans second. They have banished all visible Antillean cultural practices from the church. Having succeeded in creating one of the most solidly Antillean spaces in Paris, this group refuses to make that fact central to its practice. The contrast between these two forms of religious activism is the subject of Chapter 6.

Drawing on art, social policy, and religion, Antillean demands for both individual equality and cultural recognition confront the principles on which French national unity is constructed. Their self-definition as part of the black Atlantic challenges narrower French self-understanding, in effect creolizing French culture and society. At the same time, the rise of the extreme right, as well as racism and xenophobia in France since the 1990s, threatens to racialize debates and policies. These movements threaten the principles of individual equality that have unified the French nation, demanding instead that the nation be explicitly rooted in blood and history and excluding the growing populations of religious and ethnic minorities. Reacting to these movements, French leaders on both left and right have called for a return to the fundamental values of the Republic. The conflicts between these models highlight the difficulties involved in making the nation-state a relevant framework for identity in a globalizing—possibly postnational—world. More broadly, self-conscious efforts by ethnic activists to make identities across national boundaries challenge anthropologists and other cultural critics to rethink their own ideas about culture in ways that are less static and, perhaps like French society itself, more Creole.

CHAPTER ONE

FINDING CREOLE IDENTITIES IN MARTINIQUE AND PARIS

The View from the Hôtel L'Impératrice, Fort-de-France, Martinique

In September 1988, I was invited to speak at a luncheon of the Fort-de-France Rotary Club. Since I was beginning ethnographic field research in Martinique (see Fig. 1.1), I jumped at the chance to meet some of the city's business elite and eat a decent meal. The event took place in the restaurant of the Hôtel L'Impératrice, named for Emperor Napoleon Bonaparte's Martinican wife, Joséphine de Beauharnais, who is suspected of persuading her husband to reinstate slavery on the island. The hotel lobby—with its newsstand, tobacconist shop, café, and open view of the Savane park with its statue of Empress Joséphine, beheaded by locals in a sign of their contempt (see Fig. 1.3)— seemed like the kind of place where colonial intrigues of the sort described by Graham Greene in his novels might have taken place.

Before lunch, the ethnically mixed but all-male crowd gathered for an *apéritif* on the fourth-floor balcony. Expressing curiosity about my research, a white Frenchman warned me of the mystery and paradox of the French Antilles. Before they moved from Paris to Martinique, his wife went to see a *voyant* (fortune-teller) seeking insight into the family's fate in its new overseas endeavor. He told me this story with apparent embarrassment over his wife's breach of proper French rationality. The fortune-teller's powers to see into their fate, he said, were limited by a geocultural haze that, for her, surrounded

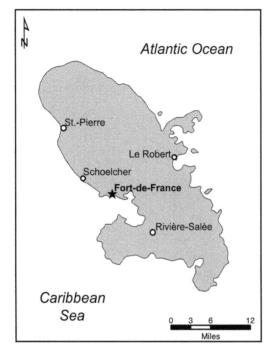

Figure 1.1   Martinique.

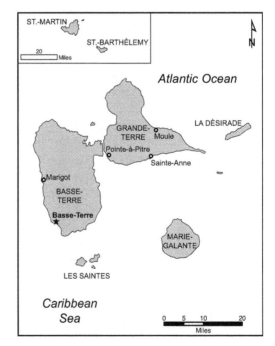

Figure 1.2   Guadeloupe.

Figure 1.3   Beheaded statue of Empress Joséphine, Fort-de-France, Martinique.
PICTURE BY MARTINIQUE-PHOTOS.COM.

Martinique. Somewhere between Africa and Europe, someplace in the Americas but not *of* the Americas, the *voyant* told his wife, adding that she could not make sense of their destination. If Martinique is not quite a distant slice of France, it is not an independent Caribbean nation either.

At the head table, I was seated with the black manager of a French utility company, an East Indian architect from Paris, an elderly black Martinican psychiatrist, and the light-skinned, possibly white club president. The *calalou de crabe*, a kind of thin gumbo with herbs and crabmeat, was made magical with the addition of a slice of *piment*, or scotch bonnet pepper. As the meal proceeded, the club president invited me to speak.

I told them of plans hatched in distant New York, something about how Martinican and Guadeloupan immigrants in Paris organize amid controversy over immigration and about their efforts to assert their distinct cultural identity in metropolitan France. When I finished, the room erupted in a lively forty-five-minute debate about Antilleans in France and the "immigrant" problem there. Many insisted that I had made a fundamental mistake. Because Martinicans are already French citizens, they asserted, they cannot be immigrants in France. They are simply moving within their own country and should be referred to as internal migrants. The distinction was important to them—immigrants, one member heatedly claimed, are foreigners, usually Arabs, who "bring their Ramadan and other crazy stuff." Martinicans are more like Corsicans, cultural insiders with a few colorful particularities. Martinicans and Guadeloupans work, they noted, in the same kinds of public service jobs that Corsicans used to hold. I asked, "But don't Antilleans suffer from racism in France?" I had read, for instance, that public housing authorities stigmatized them and applied quotas limiting their numbers. The Rotarians agreed that this had happened but insisted it was only an unfortunate mistake or misunderstanding. Arabs are the only population with problems in France, they asserted.

After lunch, four or five club members continued the discussion. One, an elderly *béké* (the local term for white plantation owners and their descendants), told me a story about a Frenchman he met sometime after World War II, an anthropologist who wanted to know about race relations in the Antilles (Leiris 1955). A black Martinican told the researcher that he, as a white metropolitan Frenchman, would have difficulty understanding the finer points of relations between the descendants of slaves and local whites. "We live here together," the black man told my predecessor, "but the *békés* do not invite us to socialize with them and we do not invite them to socialize with us. Our children do not play together. Yet we respect each other. You metropolitan whites, on the other hand, expect us to socialize with you. But you really see us as inferior." What the black man told the French anthropologist, the *béké* added with a grin, is still the way things are here.

At the research center—part of a former colonial hospital turned municipal arts center where I lived (see Fig. 1.4)—I met Marlene, a young black Martinican student who worked there as a part-time administrator. When I told her about the Rotarian lunch and the *béké*'s picture of Martinican life, she scoffed. "The *békés* don't respect us," she said. "They think everything is fine, but their racism has ruined this society."

Antilleans and the "Immigrant" Problem in France

This project began with a misunderstanding. I had lived in Paris for a few years in the early and mid-1980s. I witnessed the increasing violence and harassment against immigrants, including police shootings, beatings by gangs of "skinheads," and everyday discrimination in jobs, housing, and schools. This had become improbably personal. I had always been a beneficiary of white invisibility in the United States, yet in France I often failed to pass as an American. Something about me proclaimed "Arab" to French police. They routinely stopped and frisked me while checking my papers and asking me hostile questions, interrogations that did not happen to other Americans. One day in a café in an upscale neighborhood, sharing coffee with some

Figure 1.4   Municipal Arts Center, Fort-de-France, Martinique.

French friends, I failed to recognize myself in a mirror—who is that swarthy, slightly suspicious foreigner, I wondered. Then with sudden recognition came shock. I had begun to see myself as French people did. What about real immigrants? What did they see in the mirror?

Many immigrants could see that France was having trouble coming to terms with itself as an increasingly diverse society. The discrimination, harassment, and racism I had observed resulted in the growth of ethnic activism among immigrants and the development of immigrant rights coalitions and antiracist organizations, including, most notably, SOS Racisme, known for its evocatively named leader, Harlem Désir, and for the colorful antiracist badges it made ubiquitous in France. Shaped like an upturned hand to signal a halt to racist violence, they were inscribed with the slogan "Hands off my pal" (*Touche pas à mon pote*). SOS Racisme and other organizations used creative tactics, including cross-country marches that grabbed the attention of the press and the country. They demanded an end to racism and recognition of their cultural differences. France, they argued, must no longer be thought of as a culturally homogeneous nation. "France is like a moped; to advance it needs mixture" was a popular slogan at the time (mopeds, which are popular in Europe, run on a mix of gasoline and oil). Martinicans and Guadeloupans were prominent in these demonstrations and had assumed leadership roles in some of the largest immigrant rights and antiracist coalitions. Harlem Désir, for instance, was born in Paris of a Martinican father and French mother.

As citizens, Antilleans are not classified as immigrants and their prominence in these movements was little noticed at the time. Approximately 337,000 Martinicans and Guadeloupans live in metropolitan France, which, if they were counted as immigrants, would make them the fifth largest immigrant group, after Algerians, Portuguese, Moroccans, and Italians.[1] Antilleans would seem to be cultural insiders. They come from islands that have been part of France for over three centuries, are educated in French schools, speak French, and are deeply entrenched in French culture and society. Since they are predominantly Catholic, unlike Muslim North Africans, their religion should not stand in the way of assimilation. Recruited starting in the 1960s to work in public service jobs available only to citizens, they successfully worked in positions that, as the Rotarians had noted, Corsicans held in the past. If Antilleans faced neither cultural barriers nor legal limitations on their participation in French society, why were they now asserting difference and demanding recognition from the French state? If they were "really" French, what difference did they want to have recognized? With their centuries-long ties to French society, what did Antilleans see when they looked in the French mirror?

"But aren't these people black?" Asked in a tone that suggested it was more answer than question, this query, posed by friends and colleagues in the United States, haunted my efforts to make sense of Antilleans' cultural position in France. Although there could be no doubt that something called racism existed in France (why else would there be antiracist organizations?), there were few attempts in the early 1990s to discuss immigration or ethnicity in explicitly racial terms. Unlike Britain and the United States, France had no "race relations" literature in the social sciences. It had long been asserted that what distinguished French culture from its European neighbors was the humanist ideal according to which anyone could become French simply by accepting French culture (see Brubaker 1992; Feldblum 1999). Being French was based, as the political philosopher Ernest Renan (1992, 55) famously asserted, on consent to live in community. He explicitly rejected the idea of a French nation formed from descent or race. French society existed in a world of cultures, not races. If there was racism in France, it followed that this was a racism without races (Balibar 1991; Stolcke 1995).

At the same time, Antilleans come from societies where ideas about racial difference form an important organizing principle of social life (Giraud 1979; Murray 1997). The role of race in the French Antilles is comparable to the role it plays in the rest of the Caribbean (Alexander 1977; Martinez-Alier 1989; Segal 1993; Yelvington 1995). Antilleans may deny the relevance of race in defining who they are; one sociologist wrote that his father, "a black man from Guadeloupe," responded to harassment in France over his color or origin by pointing out, "I have been French since 1635, long before people from Nice, Savoy, Corsica or even Strasbourg" (Giraud 1985, 585).[2] Yet the very articulation of such challenges and responses implies a perception of race as visual difference from some preconceived notion of who is French. Does this mean that race is somehow hidden, but present all the same, in French culture?

Immigrant activism, by Antilleans and others, threatened the very idea of a homogeneous French culture. The emphasis on making cultural "mixture" central to French identity among immigrant activists—what we usually refer to as "diversity" in the United States—was something new for French society in the 1980s and 1990s. The French nation had been built on the idea of a unified culture, shared by all citizens. In fact, making people adopt a single culture—turning peasants into Frenchmen—was a central objective in both France and the colonies of its former empire (Weber 1976; Bancel et al. 2003). I began to think that the "immigrant problem" was not about immigration. It was a "French problem," defined by French ideas about different cultures, by hidden assumptions about race and French policies toward people designated as different, as "immigrants." The French had made immigrants into the "immigrant problem," as Jean-Paul Sartre (1954) would have said, creating a category defined more by French social concerns than by the lives of the people thus categorized.

The demands that Antilleans and other immigrants made for cultural recognition ignited a national debate in France about the meaning of being French and the organization of French society. The very structure of the French state has long been marked by the assumption that class and class conflict are fundamental to the organization of society. Public policy, as well as social science, has been organized around the idea that le social, as class-related policy debates are known in France, was the basic reality behind politics. Immigrant demands for cultural recognition, the formation of recognizably distinct cultural communities, and the rise of a kind of multiculturalism in French society has, since the 1980s, become central to French political life, raising the possibility that culture—le culturel—may be in the process of replacing the social as the central structuring principle of French society.

Antilleans provided an ideal group for testing this hypothesis. Despite their insider status, these black French citizens had determined to demand something that had never been available in France—the right to be full citizens and, at the same time, maintain a distinct identity. This demand seemed especially ironic in the Antillean case, since in 1946 Martinique and Guadeloupe had explicitly opted to become departments of France, rather than independent countries. Yet having once chosen assimilation, postcolonial Antilleans in France now desired difference. Because legally they were not immigrants, their turn toward cultural activism cannot be attributed to their status as "foreigners." The ways Antilleans worked toward asserting their distinctiveness—drawing on notions of Antillean and French culture—promised to provide useful insights into the meaning of the concept of culture in a postcolonial world.

In both Martinique and metropolitan France, government officials and all sorts of activists regularly deploy ideas about culture in order to make claims about who belongs in various groups and to argue for public policies. They often invoke the term "culture" in ways that seem to reflect anthropological usage. *Culture*, when used in France, covers a multitude of objects, from art to peasant life and rituals to housing and festivals associated with the industrial working class. It is used in ways that resemble a reified version of the anthropological notion of a total way of life, in which people do not "have" culture so much as they are had by it. While "culture" is often used to link a group of people with a set of practices and a territory, the manner in which that linkage is made and the content and meaning of any given set of practices is still controversial in France. This is especially the case in discussions of the cultures of immigrants, whose behavior is often held up by French intellectuals against an ideal type of the culture of their societies of origin, and of immigrant youth, who are frequently referred to as being *entre deux cultures*, between two cultures (Hargreaves 1996; Wacquant 1993). Because the French term is the same as the English word "culture," in what follows I will use italics when I am referring to the French vernacular.

The fact that the very terms and concepts of traditional anthropological analysis—especially culture but also "race" and "racism"—have become self-conscious elements in debates about French society, raises questions about how anthropologists and other social scientists can continue to use them. What, for instance, is "culture" in a context of self-conscious creation and assertion of identities? What is "race," and does it make sense to talk about it in a society where the very notion has been banished from public discourse? What, in that context, do people mean by racism? How does the experience of racism shape people's self-definition in terms of race and culture? Is French national *culture* really open to any "immigrant" who wishes to assimilate, or do French ideas about cultural differences—especially the differences of dark-skinned people from the former French empire—mean that some people can never become truly French? Has *culture* in France taken on some of the deterministic qualities of race? These became some of the central questions guiding my research.[3]

POSTCOLONIAL MARTINIQUE:
A LAND WITHOUT HISTORY OR A CULTURAL HOMELAND?

Concerned that my years in Paris had dulled my sense of the nonordinary, I decided to begin my research in Martinique. I needed culture shock, something to reset my sights on aspects of Antillean life in France that insiders take for granted. In the fall of 1988, I boarded a small Liat propeller plane that island-hopped from Puerto Rico to Antigua and Dominica, each runway getting dangerously shorter as the plane flew across the Caribbean. When we arrived in Martinique, the Lamentin airport, a few kilometers outside of Fort-de-France, appeared small, old-fashioned, and nothing like the international airports of Paris. If the details of officialdom—customs officers and documents, for instance—were clearly French, other aspects of life suggested that I was not in Paris anymore. I found housing in a center for researchers located in a former colonial hospital surrounded by a tropical garden unlike anything I had seen in France. The nearby produce market highlighted Martinique's distance from Europe. There I found men selling big green and orange coconuts from piles on the ground or from the backs of trucks (see Fig. 1.5). Using machetes, they would deftly cut a hole in the fruit so their customers could drink the milk. Cafés expected customers to make their own *ti'punch* (a popular local mixture of rum, lime, and sugar), leaving the bottle of rum—typically 62 percent alcohol smelling distinctly like petrol—on the table along with sugar, lime, and a carafe of water.

Figure 1.5   Selling coconuts in Fort-de-France.

In addition to culture shock, I suspected that I would find the roots of An-tillean political activism there. Martinique is a paradox, the birthplace of prominent figures in twentieth-century anticolonial struggles, such as Frantz Fanon and Aimé Césaire, yet still part of France. On the advice of colleagues, I had immersed myself in novels by French Antillean writers, including Joseph Zobel, Edouard Glissant, Maryse Condé, Simone Schwartz-Bart, Raphaël Confiant, and Patrick Chamoiseau. That such a large body of cre-ative work came out of these small islands suggested a lively political and in-tellectual life there—a land of intellectual giants, locked in struggle with the waning French empire, I fantasized.

Martinique and Guadeloupe are no longer referred to as colonies. In 1946 they became French *départements d'outre-mer* (overseas departments).[4] Most of the same institutions, from the *préfet* (the local representative of the cen-tral government) to the schools, that exist in any French department also exist in the Antilles. If colonial domination was founded on violence, post-colonial domination now works, in Martinique, through other forms of per-suasion, including substantial economic subsidies, education, and the overwhelming presence of French cultural institutions.[5] I wondered if the fa-mous French assimilation machine, the policies and practices that had made French citizens out of the diverse peoples of France, had erased Martinique's cultural specificity. Would I find the cultural and political descendants of rev-olutionary Antillean writers like Fanon and Césaire or the assimilated resi-dents of a "typical" French province, distinct from Bordeaux or Brest only by their distance from Paris?[6]

Weather forecasts on the radio in Martinique signaled the centrality of metropolitan France to Martinican life. They were more likely to report driv-ing conditions in the Alps than storms in the Caribbean. A few days after I ar-rived, an unannounced tropical storm swept in unexpectedly, flooding streets and bringing life to a halt. For many Martinicans, the spread of French ideas and practices was like the storm itself, washing away any local sense of self along with most local practices. Strolling around the Savane (the city's lush twelve-and-a-half-acre park) in the evening, I saw young people fashionably dressed in the clothes Paris had made the gold standard of world fashion. Many expensive automobiles filled the narrow streets of Fort-de-France. The conspicuous display of wealth seemed to contradict the high unemployment rates.[7] Teachers, police, customs agents, and the many other Martinicans em-ployed by the French government benefit from a 40 percent increase in salary over standard metropolitan French rates to compensate for the expense of life in the Antilles, while many others receive benefits from the generous French welfare state. These high salaries and subsidies supported a consumption style that looked far more French than Caribbean. Eighty percent of the goods consumed in the French Antilles are imported, an ironic situation for islands whose colonization was long based on the production of goods for export to Europe. Martinicans linked consumer goods and their public display to French ideas of modernity.

Christian Bertin, an artist I met at the Service municipal d'action culturelle (SERMAC), took me to a school in a working-class neighborhood.[8] The school was bright and open, with comfortable little classrooms (see Fig. 1.6). In one corner of the spacious playground, Christian showed me a little playhouse his students had decorated with large bunches of raspberries, a fruit not indigenous to Martinique (see Fig. 1.7). Even the Antilleans' imagination has been colonized; that they draw on "foreign" fruits instead of local produce symbolizes their alienation from the local, Christian claimed, and leads to poor results in school. Children exposed to "European images," as he called them, fail to understand the core of their native culture.

Yet even for cultural activists like Christian, French culture is seductive. After four years of art studies in France, he found it difficult to return to Martinique. He constantly felt the pull of Paris, as if France represented access to "real culture" in a way that Martinique did not. Although he recognized that the cultures of Martinique and France are intimately linked, Christian insisted that local distinctiveness should be maintained. Through his art and teaching, he was committed to building a strong sense of what he called *antillanité*, or "Caribbeanness." Based on the work of Edouard Glissant, *antillanité*

Figure 1.6   School, Fort-de-France.

Figure 1.7   Playhouse decorated by students, Fort-de-France.

focuses on two equally important principles. First, the Martinican economy should be rebuilt with a focus on local production and trade within the Caribbean. Second, artistic production and education must be grounded in popular culture. More than "mere folklore," art linked to everyday life would be the first step toward the production of a national identity not subordinate to France (see Glissant 1981, 178, 183).

Language is, not surprisingly, at the heart of this effort to assert a Martinican national identity. Most Martinicans are bilingual—they speak Creole but they have been educated in French, the language of government and business. I had read a great deal about efforts to legitimize Creole as a language equal to French in Martinique and had contacted Jean Bernabé and Lambert-Félix Prudent, two linguists and Creole-language activists, upon my arrival (see Bébel-Gisler 1976; Prudent 1983; Prudent 1993; Schnepel 1993). They put me in touch with Paul Blameble, a middle school teacher in the north of Martinique who had, with a colleague, organized courses in Creole for several years. Paul's students were mostly the children of agricultural workers from families that used Creole as the dominant language at home. French law requires that French be used in most subjects in the public schools, but since 1982 regional languages have been taught as a distinct subject. Drawing on pedagogical experiments in Guadeloupe, Paul and his colleague developed their Creole curriculum after that law was passed. But they faced a problem:

parents did not want their children studying Creole at school. At meetings with teachers, parents would argue that their children already knew Creole and that, in any case, Creole was not a serious subject. It would only prepare their children for careers as vulgar ruffians. Paul and his colleague gradually persuaded the parents that Creole would enhance their children's education, drawing on research that showed the enhanced school success of children educated in Creole. That it should be so difficult to persuade Martinicans of the value of their own language, Paul noted, shows the depth of their cultural alienation.

I encountered similar concerns with the affirmation of cultural identity among labor leaders. Daniel Marie-Sainte, one of the leaders of the Centrale Syndicale des Travailleurs Martiniquais (CSTM, Union of Martinican Workers), the largest "independentist" (*indépendantiste*) trade union, explained the threat to local identity represented by the growth of "big box" French retail. Firms like Conforama, a large distributor of furniture and appliances, attracted Martinican consumers through its relatively affordable and distinctly "modern" goods. These imported enterprises drove Martinican artisans, unable to compete, out of business, creating unemployment and guaranteeing the loss of local craft traditions. Ecologists cited the threat of tourist development for coastal ecology and linked the growth of tourism to the demise of traditional culture, portraying Martinican culture as the equivalent of a fragile ecosystem. These fears were crystallized in the theme song of the 1990 Carnival—"Le gran méchan lou" (the Big Bad Wolf), by Djo Dezormo—which referred to the impending transformation of the European Union into a single open market. The song put into a danceable rhythm a theme I often heard expressed in conversations with Martinicans—that Europe, led by France, would "devour" the helpless Antilles, attached despite themselves to the unified European economy.

Beginning in the 1980s, many of the concerns expressed by teachers, language activists, ecologists, and union leaders found expression in a political and literary movement called *créolité*. Announced in a manifesto by Martinican novelists Patrick Chamoiseau and Raphaël Confiant and linguist Jean Bernabé, the movement asserted that Caribbean societies represent a kind of cultural avant-garde. Declaring that Martinicans and Guadeloupans were neither "European, African, nor Asian," they proclaimed themselves to be Creole (Bernabé et al. 1989, 13). Martinicans needed to work, they claimed, to preserve their own traditions and study the history of the development of their own culture (Bernabé et al. 1989, 34, 37). What characterizes Martinican and other Caribbean societies, they argued, is a capacity to make the contributions of outsiders, including the French government, their own. Just as their ancestors had taken African and European languages and created an entirely new language—Creole—Caribbean societies were characterized, the manifesto writers insisted, by a capacity to creolize the practices and resources people tried to impose on them from the outside.[9] Instead of being assimilated into French culture, the Creole cultures of the Antilles transformed that culture, in the Caribbean, into something new. This capacity might serve as a defense against the decline of local traditions and practices.

I had gone to Martinique to find the source of Antillean political activism and to learn about Martinican political culture. What I found was a country in which *culture* itself had become the main object of political action. The self-conscious assertion of Martinican identity in the context of French colonialism is not new—in the 1930s Aimé Césaire made identity central to his anticolonial poetry and theater. From Césaire's *négritude* movement to the more recent ideals of *antillanité* and *créolité*, literature and art have been central to the assertion of a distinct Martinican identity. In the past few decades, activists have expanded their focus to include the promotion of the Creole language, the revival of "popular" musical styles, such as Guadeloupan *gwoka* and Martinican *bélè*, and the ethnographic study and representation, in books and museums, of "traditional" housing, crafts, and clothing (Giraud 1997, 386; Price 1998). Once limited to the independentist side of Martinican politics, efforts to educate the Martinican public about its *culture* have become central objectives across the local political spectrum (Daniel 2002; Miles 1999). For Martinican political leaders and activists, the social and political health of the island depends on the successful transformation of Martinicans into "cultural citizens" who are well grounded in the island's history and knowledgeable about its territory, traditions, and language (Murray 2002, 53).

These efforts to assert Martinican specificity occur in a context in which French practices and institutions are increasingly present. Drawing on four decades of observation in Martinique, Richard Price observes that "it is as if the massive steamroller of French (post)colonialism, with its destructive bending of consciousness and identity, has finally made a sweep through even the most rural, least modern areas of the island" (1998, 172). Some activists fear that efforts to make the cultural education of the population central to political life will turn Martinicans into spectators of their own culture and turn the culture into a kind of commodity (Giraud 1999; Réno 1997; Price 1998). The assertion of Martinican cultural specificity and debates about it shaped in the shadow of French economic and cultural power have become central issues of Martinican political and economic life. Relations between the Antilles and France, as I soon learned in France, stand as a kind of metaphor for thinking about the place of Antilleans in the *métropole*—the term used to distinguish continental France from its overseas possessions.

ANTILLEAN DIFFERENCE AND DIFFERENCES IN PARIS

Antilleans often say that Paris is a cold city. Several young men I knew in Martinique told me that they had prepared themselves for emigration by working in cold storage facilities—readying themselves for the Parisian climate. Their perception of the city's coldness also comes from the size of the metropolitan area and the relative isolation of Antilleans from one another. With approximately 10 million people, the population of Paris is ten times greater than that of Martinique and Guadeloupe combined. The majority of Antilleans in metropolitan France live in Paris, mostly in the city's working-class neighborhoods and suburbs (see Fig. 1.8). Half of the Antilleans in France live in moderate income public housing, but they do not form a majority in any neighborhood or town in the region (Marie 1993a, 12). Many work in the public sector, in local administrations, customs, the postal service, hospitals, and public transportation. I made useful contacts in Fort-de-France in a few days and, as noted above, within a few weeks I could hardly cross the city without encountering people who recognized me. Establishing

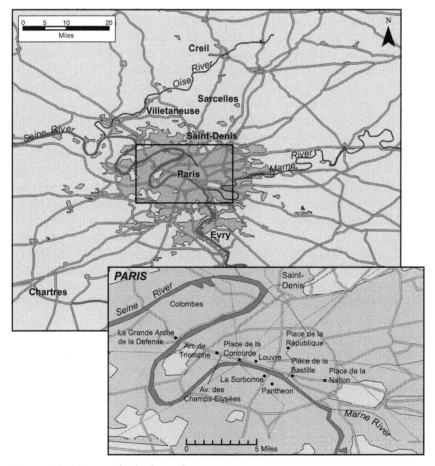

Figure 1.8   Paris and suburbs, with city center inset.

myself in Paris would take considerably longer, an experience I shared with many Antilleans, as I was soon to discover.

Most migrants from the Antilles use contacts with family and friends to ease their adaptation to life in Paris. For me, contacts from Martinique, as well as people I had met during earlier trips to France, proved essential in orienting my research in Paris. Jean Galap, a Martinican social scientist and social activist, invited me to meetings of the association he had helped organize and informed me of events where I was likely to meet other Antillean activists. Father Pierre Lacroix, a Guadeloupan priest who ran a Catholic center for Antilleans in Paris, also invited me to meetings of groups at the center, while providing helpful suggestions on how to find Antilleans in Paris. From previous visits, I knew that the Agence nationale pour l'insertion et la promotion des travailleurs d'outre-mer (ANT, or National Agency for the Promotion and Insertion of Workers from Overseas) had published a catalog of Antillean associations in France (ANT 1985, 1988). For Antilleans in France, and for me as a researcher, the mainstream French media, as well as Antillean media in France, often provide a curious reflection of their lives, focusing on "hot" nightclubs and restaurants or troubled working-class neighborhoods where they live and the "exotic" islands from which they come.

My first few months in Paris were spent interviewing anyone who would talk to me, following leads provided by my initial contacts and the media. These included government bureaucrats (especially at the ANT), artists, intellectuals, leaders of professional associations, members of student groups and sports clubs. I attended dozens of community events, from *zouk* parties to literary conferences and from government press conferences to dry policy planning sessions with local associations. As I attended meetings and interviewed people, my list of contacts grew and I began to get a broad sense of the experiences in France that inspired Antillean demands for cultural recognition.

In March 1989, I attended a performance by an Antillean theater troupe in the municipal auditorium of Colombes, a working-class Paris suburb. The association, Eloge, is based in Paris and was invited to Colombes to perform for a local Antillean group.[10] Prior to the show, the town's mayor addressed the two groups as part of his reelection campaign. The mayor opened the event by speaking briefly about his personal attachment to Martinique and Guadeloupe, mentioning that he had always enjoyed his vacations there. In a patronizing tone, he noted that these experiences had led him to the belief that Antilleans possess a "fine and interesting culture" and that it is important to "respect" that culture. This position of respect, he added, is the very opposite of a racist attitude unmindful of cultural differences. In fact, he noted, it is preferable to speak of Antilleans as a cultural group and stay away from references to race, avoiding the use of terms such as *noir* (black). This observation, in turn, provided a platform for the mayor to denounce the candidate of the far-right National Front. Then he opened the floor for questions.

The Antillean audience responded with heated questions, demanding to know why their clubs and teams were not permitted to use the town's public facilities—including the meeting hall and the soccer fields—as often as other groups. They wanted to know what the mayor was likely to do for Antilleans in the community. Perhaps, members of the audience stated, denial of access to municipal facilities stems from racism at city hall. To this the mayor responded vehemently. "You are all my constituents," he said, "and I have a published program that lists the ways I will serve the interests of this town. But as Antilleans you cannot make special demands." "On the other hand," he added, "as a group you do cause specific problems with your habit of noisy parties and loud music in public housing." "I realize," he said, "that you are fun loving and boisterous, but you must control yourselves better."

The president of the local Antillean association stood and, in an offended tone, pointed out that if public halls were made available to Antillean associations more often, there would be less need for parties at home. The mayor, still ruffled, demanded to know if the audience thought racism was a problem in "his" town. Perhaps there is not much overt racism here, someone responded, a statement that left lingering doubts about the hidden effects of racism in city hall and elsewhere in France. For the mayor, however, this provided conclusive proof of the quality of life in the town, a confirmation of his good nonracist work. Racism could not be a problem for Antilleans, he added, since they are French citizens, not immigrants. Ethnicity or cultural distinctiveness is not subject to racism. Perhaps not, someone in the crowd noted, but many French people cannot tell one black person from another; they cannot distinguish an African from an Antillean. Finally one of the audience members declared, "We represent a cultural group here and as such we feel that we have been neglected." As he left, the mayor gruffly dismissed their complaints: "I have been mayor for twenty-five years and I know what is going on in my town."

This exchange led me to rethink my own approach to the concepts of race, ethnicity, and racism—commonsense folk terms and analytic concepts employed by citizens and social scientists in both the United States and France. I was beginning to understand that the categories and processes used to classify people into groups in France differ from those used in the United States. There is a growing consensus in the scientific community that race is meaningless as a biological categorization of humans and is only useful as a social construct. However, the American public does not share this view, and race remains, for many Americans, a self-evident way of categorizing and evaluating people.[11] What exactly did French people and Antilleans mean when they invoked these concepts?[12] Why did the mayor believe that the invocation of race was necessarily racist but ethnicity could not be subject to racism?

The audience and the mayor disagreed sharply about the place of ethnic distinctiveness in French society. The mayor's view represents what has been called "neorepublican discourse" in French politics—an ideology that calls for the cultural assimilation of immigrants and blames the cultures of the immigrants for any failure to assimilate.[13] The Antillean audience viewed cultural diversity in France—especially their own—as a given. For them, the mayor's willingness to invoke ethnicity to praise far-away islands and condemn boisterous parties seemed selective. Why not take ethnicity into account when providing municipal services? Was this selective invocation of cultural difference what they meant when they spoke of racism?

Creole Identities in Postcolonial Paris

Direct encounters between Antilleans and French politicians were rare. Given their dispersal in the region, however, organized events that brought Antilleans together—parties, conferences, concerts, and association meetings—were central to creating a sense of community among themselves. Antilleans engage in a wide variety of organized activities; choosing which to study required determining which activities seemed representative. It also required patience and luck. For a few months, I practiced with a soccer team affiliated with the association of Antillean subway workers. Although the players and coach were welcoming, it soon became clear that I was not up to their level of play (a great understatement), and standing on the sidelines did not seem like an effective way to gather information (see Fig. 1.9). Then I became a dues-paying member of an association of Antillean postal workers, only to find that they had no meetings and organized no events over the next year.

A few months after I arrived in Paris, a friend put me in touch with the leader of a new association whose objective, I was told, was to remake the image of Antilleans in France. Bringing together artists, musicians, singers, and fashion designers, the group intended to forgo nostalgic re-creations of life in the Antilles and the stereotypical and highly commercial sound of *zouk* music in favor of art and performances that reflected the lives of Antilleans in France. This idea intrigued me, so I called Jean-Pierre Clément, the leader of the group, and he invited me to meet him at a rehearsal of their choral group. Instead of getting the interview I expected, I was recruited to sing by the group's musical director. I quickly discovered that this group's objectives were not its only unique characteristic. While most of the members were Antilleans, many, like Maryse Carbet, a young actress, were born in France of Antillean parents.

In her mid-twenties when we met, Maryse was the light-skinned daughter of a mixed marriage. Her father was an engineer from Martinique and her mother a housewife from northern France. Raised in a working-class suburb of Paris, Maryse and her sister learned to think of themselves as culturally white, like their mother. Creole, their father's first language, was never spoken

Figure 1.9   Soccer match, featuring a visiting team from Martinique, brings out an Antillean crowd.

at home and little mention was made of Antillean culture. At home, her parents played only classical music—a symbol of "pure" European culture, unlike, for instance, jazz or Caribbean music.[14] They were concerned that their daughters, if exposed to two different cultures, would be confused and ill adapted to life in France. But the working-class neighborhood they lived in was full of immigrants of many origins. While their relatively higher social standing made her something of an outsider in her neighborhood, Maryse began to question her origins and think about the mirror in which she was reflected.

Soon after moving to Paris in pursuit of her acting career, Maryse started dating a young Jewish Frenchman who introduced her to ways of being ethnic and French simultaneously. Their circle of friends included many Africans, who accused her of being too white and denying her "real" identity as a black person. Maryse left behind her Jewish boyfriend and began seeing a man from Cameroon who took her to ethnographic films about Africa. Her acting career began to blossom, but at the expense of her growing sense of cultural identity. Much to her chagrin, she was frequently cast as the "exotic woman"—a North African, an Antillean, or sometimes an African—but never as white. Maryse took this as a sign to turn from Africa to the Caribbean, and she stopped seeing the man from Cameroon.

Maryse's mother had discouraged her children's connections to Martinique. Maryse had visited the island only once as a child, but her adult determination to explore her roots led her to spend two months there with her grandmother in 1988. To Maryse, Martinicans looked amazingly secure in their identity, something she had never felt. When I met her, she had been back from Martinique for a few months and was in the middle of defining herself vis-à-vis that society. She believed she would always be an outsider in Martinique. "I have too much French culture," she noted, pointing to all the French literature that lined her bookshelves. She was continually dissatisfied with what she called Jean-Pierre's "Martinican" work ethic. He improvises too much, she said, while I am "Cartesian" and systematic. He was more "authentically" Caribbean. Eventually she began to think of herself as a Martinican with deep roots in France.

Like many other Antilleans in France, Maryse did not intend to become fully Martinican. Rather, she wanted to find a way to make Martinican identity part of a broader sense of self. In the spirit of the sort of postmodern positioning that blurs the line between the anthropologist and the members of the culture under study, she borrowed my Creole language tapes to study the language. She read widely, including much of the Antillean literature I had read while preparing for fieldwork. Maryse immersed herself in the novels and manifestoes of the *créolité* writers who insisted on the multiple sources—African, European, Indian—of Martinican society. They portrayed a Martinican culture that was continually in a process of development and change. Thus, to be Creole in the terms of this movement was to move beyond the narrow confines of race and nation into something new (Bernabé et al. 1989). Maryse saw her own life reflected in this idea of a new multicultural, multiracial person, rooted in Martinique but also France.

IS IT POSSIBLE TO BE ANTILLEAN IN FRANCE?

When he heard I wanted to research Antillean emigrants in France, Marc Pulvar, a leader of the independentist CSTM union in Martinique raised an eyebrow and asked, "Antilleans or Martinicans?" "Here we are Martinicans—touchy nationalists too," he chuckled. In France, however, I discovered that distinctions between the two Caribbean islands faded away. For most French people, Martinicans and Guadeloupans were just Antilleans.[15]

Yet if Martinicans and Guadeloupans become Antilleans in France, they also become "black." Instead of attending to the nuances of descent or shades of skin current in the Caribbean, French policymakers, along with employers, landlords, and police, lump Antilleans with Africans and other immigrants. Despite their legal status and their socialization into French culture, their categorization with immigrants makes it impossible for Antilleans in France to claim that they are simply French. They are linked by origin and skin color to the kinds of people who, in the French view, are unable to adopt French culture. They become immigrants, part of the "immigrant problem" in French society.

Antilleans in metropolitan France are faced with a basic question: Is it possible to be Antillean in France? Talking with Maryse and others, I began to understand that my object of study, "Antilleans in France," could not be defined solely by place of birth or descent. The Antilleans I met did not adhere to a set of cultural practices that could be simply defined as "Antillean." They had not turned to a primordial ethnic identity, transposed and updated from the cultures of Martinique and Guadeloupe. Martinique and Guadeloupe are the cultural hinterland for Antilleans in Paris. In France, however, they were challenged to invent an Antillean identity that had never existed in the islands. As they worked to be equal citizens and to be recognized as culturally distinct, Antilleans used art, social policy, and religion to shape their identity in ways recognizably French in form but Caribbean in substance. As I observed and participated in the activities of associations Antilleans formed in France, I began to understand the broader ways in which difference was represented in French society. In taking up the challenge to invent themselves as Antillean, Antilleans in France also began to reinvent what it meant to be French.

Notes

1. Marie 2002, 32; Boëldieu and Borrel 2000, 2. The Antillean population includes both those born in the Antilles and anyone born in France of a parent born in the Antilles. Because they are French citizens, they are not included in data about immigrants. The total immigrant population in France in 1999, excluding Antilleans, was 4.3 million, or about 7.4 percent of the total population. The total DOM-TOM population residing in metropolitan France in 1990, counting people born in or descended from people born in all of France's overseas departments and territories (in addition to Guadeloupe and Martinique, this includes French Guiana, Réunion and a few other places), was 526,512 (Marie 1993a, 15). This constitutes a substantial population of color but, as I have noted, is not counted as part of the immigrant population in France.

2. "Notre père, un nègre de la Guadeloupe, a coutume de rétorquer à ceux qui, en France, l'importunent au sujet de sa couleur ou de son origine: 'Je suis Français depuis 1635, bien avant les Niçois, les Savoyards, les Corses ou même les Strasbourgeois.'" Unless otherwise indicated, I am responsible for all translations.

3. The question of how to continue to use "culture" in a world where it is increasingly deployed as a self-conscious element of identity construction—identity being a similarly slippery folk and scientific concept—has been addressed by a number of anthropologists. Analyses especially relevant to the arguments I am making here include Abu-Lughod 1991; Appadurai 1991; Baumann 1996; Greenhouse and Greenwood 1998; Hall 2002; Handler 1988; Herzfeld 1992; Stolcke 1995; and van Beek 2000. I address the history of these questions in France in Chapter 2.

4. Because they are not independent, the French Antilles are often compared to Puerto Rico. But their status as overseas departments is closer to that of a state. A better comparison, as Katherine Browne (2002, 376) has pointed out, is with Hawaii.

5. See Chamoiseau 1997 for a local analysis of how this works.

6. Whether or not "typical French provinces" can in some way be defined as uniformly French is controversial. See Rogers 1991 for an ethnographic example of how regional cultures fit within national culture in France and Rogers 2001 for an overview of French anthropological research related to this question.

7. Thirty percent or higher since the 1980s. Lamia Oualalou, "Le premier ministre arrive ce soir en Martinique; L'économie antillaise à la dérive," *Le Figaro*, October 27, 1999. See also Browne 2002.

8. The SERMAC, as its name indicates, is funded by the city of Fort-de-France as well as the Regional Council. It organizes major arts festivals and well-attended arts courses throughout the year. David Murray (2002) has written extensively about the work of the SERMAC and its role in identity debates in Martinique.

9. The *créolité* movement draws on ideas developed in the social science creolization debates. A useful critique of *créolité* can be found in Price and Price 1997. Recent reviews of the literature on creolization include Khan 2001; Yelvington 2001; and Price 2001a. See Réno 1997 for an analysis of creolization in Martinican politics.

10. "Eloge" is a pseudonym. I have used pseudonyms for most people and organizations in this book, except in the case of public figures whose work I cite and activists who specifically requested that I use their real names.

11. Regarding science perspectives on race, see Templeton 1999. Regarding American "common sense" on race, see Dominguez 1986; Omi and Winant 1986.

12. See Wacquant 1993; Baumann 1996; Brown 1998 for analyses that explore the ways people invoke these concepts in different societies.

13. On neorepublican discourse in France, see Chapter 2, as well as Favell 1997; Wieviorka 1997; Weil and Crowley 1994; Hargreaves and McKinney 1997.

14. The Guyanese poet Léon Gontron Damas's poem "Hiccups" seems reflected in this story. See Damas 1972, 38; Kennedy 1975 for an English translation.

15. Technically the term "Antilles" refers, in both French and English, to all the islands of the Caribbean. But in France, when people mention the Antilles, they mean only Martinique and Guadeloupe.

Further Reading

Baumann, Gerd. 1996. *Contesting Culture: Discourses of Identity in Multi-Ethnic London*. Cambridge: Cambridge University Press. This ethnography of the ways people create and assert ethnic identities in one part of London provides an interesting comparison with ethnic activism in France.

Hall, Kathleen. 2002. *Lives in Translation: Sikh Youth as British Citizens*. Philadelphia: University of Pennsylvania Press. This ethnographic account of the cultural politics surrounding British identity and citizenship for the children of Sikh immigrants shows how immigrants and their children are contributing to changes in how Europeans think about national identity.

Price, Richard. 1998. *The Convict and the Colonel*. Boston: Beacon. Price combines the strange story of one Martinican, the history of an election day uprising in 1925, and his own long-term experience in Martinique in an analysis of postcolonial transformations of Martinican culture and society since the 1960s.

Stovall, Tyler, and Georges Van Den Abbeele, eds. 2003. *French Civilization and Its Discontents: Nationalism, Colonialism, Race*. Lanham, Md.: Lexington. An interdisciplinary collection of essays focusing on the making of French identities in colonial and postcolonial contexts, including several that examine the French Antilles.

CHAPTER TWO

WHAT IS THE
PRICE OF FRENCHNESS?

THE NATION ON PARADE

The bicentennial of the French Revolution was observed in 1989, and Bastille Day (July 14) was celebrated with more than the usual vigor. The French government hosted the annual summit of the leaders of the Group of Seven leading industrialized nations (as it was called) that July, and thirty-five other heads of state and government had been invited to attend the festivities as well. Working under the direction of President François Mitterrand, the planners organized the celebrations around the idea that the French Revolution had been the founding act of modern times, signaling the end of feudalism and the birth of the ideals of democracy and human rights in the world.[1]

The festivities began with French celebrities reading, in front of the assembled world leaders, the Declaration of the Rights of Man and of the Citizen, part of the constitution of every French republic since 1789. Over the course of the celebrations and the summit, the guests participated in the inauguration of three of the largest architectural and arts projects in twentieth-century Paris—the Bastille Opera, the expanded Louvre, and Arche de la Défense. One journalist observed that the bicentennial celebration had turned Paris into a gigantic theater that connected the ideals of the French Revolution, the spread of democracy and human rights, and Mitterrand's monumental building projects.[2]

The high point was a massive parade on the evening of July 14. Performers from all over the world marched along the traditional Bastille Day parade route down the Champs-Elysées and around the Place de la Concorde, where 10,000 invited guests were seated. A group of Chinese students dressed in red and black marched first, in silence, behind a banner reading "We Carry On," which commemorated the unsuccessful student uprising in Beijing two months earlier. Several hundred musicians and marchers dressed to represent the prerevolutionary French provinces came next, followed by section after section of performers and musicians from many different countries—a Festival of the Planet's Tribes, according to the parade's organizers. Nearly a million people crowded the parade route, while millions more worldwide watched on television.

France's revolution was represented as an event with a double meaning. For France, it defined the foundation of the nation, symbolized in the title of the spectacle—La Marseillaise—and in the gathering of marchers from the diverse prerevolutionary provinces into one unified bloc. The French Revolution also signaled the start of "modernity," spreading the ideals of democracy, freedom, and human rights throughout the world. This was why representatives of all nations joined the celebrations as both spectators and participants. In the parade's symbolism, France stood for the unity of the world brought together by the "universal" values of the French Revolution.

The spectacle can also be interpreted as a celebration of hierarchy born of cultural differences. Some sections of the parade celebrated aspects of French identity, promoting elements of regional or class folkways in which all French people could see their collective heritage made visible. Floats and marching groups drew on scenes from French cinema and literature. For instance, one float re-created a scene from the film La bête humaine, an enormous locomotive driven by a soot-smeared man resembling the actor Jean Gabin. This classic representation of the French industrial working classes inspired one journalist to remark, "This is who we are . . . in some way, we are all Gabin."[3] Another float, pulled by white men dressed in colonial uniforms—complete with pith helmets—carried a well-known African musician conducting a drum orchestra. The float was surrounded by bare-breasted dancing black women. Seeing this, a television commentator remarked that drums are the first instrument of children, the communication device of primitives, and the favored method to call people to revolution. Standing in the center of the vast Place de la Concorde, draped with an enormous French flag, the American soprano Jessye Norman closed the show with the French national anthem. A newspaper described her as the "absolute, imperial soprano of all the world's ghetto mothers . . . exuberant tenderness."[4]

The events of Bastille Day 1989 provided a public display of the tension between two aspects of French identity. To be French is to be a member of the nation whose heritage is the French Revolution, a nation of individual citizens of the Republic. The values promoted by the Republic are to be understood as universal human values that can be applied to all people. At the same time, many non-French performers in the spectacle represented other societies. They were there to celebrate French accomplishments, to which they might aspire but had yet to achieve. To be French is to be a member of a particular nation and a representative of a universal ideal. To be anything else is to be only particular, a condition that may be escaped only by becoming French.

WHOSE BICENTENNIAL?

The Bastille Day festivities were the high point in a year of conferences, parades, and spectacles commemorating the founding event of modern France. It was an opportunity for the French government to dramatically restate the values of the Republic as well as assert the idea that France, by virtue of its revolutionary heritage, continued to play an important role in the world. While most people in France were swept up in the excitement of the moment, not everyone understood the bicentennial in the same way. There were objections to commemorating the revolution without recognizing that it had included dictatorship and terror. There were small groups who denounced what they saw as a celebration of regicide. Representatives of the Catholic Church expressed doubts about the Revolution's anticlerical legacy. These objections were swept aside by President Mitterrand, who asserted that the overwhelming majority of French people saw the Revolution as their heritage.[5]

Many of the Antillean activists I knew in France had mixed feelings about the bicentennial. President Mitterrand was popular among Antilleans. The day he was inaugurated to his first term as president in 1981, he went to the Pantheon in Paris, where many of France's national heroes are buried. There he placed a rose on the tomb of Victor Schoelcher, a nineteenth-century French politician who was instrumental in ending slavery in the colonies. But the definitive end of slavery in the French Antilles did not occur until 1848, long after the Revolution of 1789. The bicentennial commemorated a revolution that promised equality to all but failed to deliver on that promise.

I first became aware of the difficulties Antilleans had with seeing their own history in the celebration of the French Revolution at a conference organized in March 1989—four months before the bicentennial parade—by an association promoting the creation of an Antillean-oriented community radio station in France. Held at a university that specialized in Latin American studies in Paris, the event brought together many leading Antillean intellectuals and French sympathizers. The evening's featured speaker was Henri Bangou, the mayor of Pointe à Pitre in Guadeloupe, and the author of a book about the French Revolution and slavery in Guadeloupe (Bangou 1989).[6] Introducing Bangou, one of the organizers pointed out that few of the official bicentennial events in France focused on or even mentioned the colonies or slavery. "If we want to know who we are," he said, "we have to know our own history." Bangou's book and lecture, he said, would provide insights into both.

Over the course of his talk, Bangou analyzed the course of the 1789 Revolution in Paris and the Caribbean colonies. The Declaration of the Rights of Man and of the Citizen, voted into law in 1789, asserted the equality of all men. Slavery, he noted, should have ended with that declaration. But the French bourgeoisie had grown rich on the triangular trade and they, along with their colonial allies, resisted efforts to end slavery in the colonies.[7] Over the next five years, debates in France would lead to formal equality for "free men of color," the mixed-race descendants of Europeans and slaves. However, Bangou pointed out, the slaves themselves had to convince the French revolutionaries to end slavery.

The Revolution in France triggered turmoil in its Caribbean possessions. Conflicts between whites and free men of color over political equality were one element of that turmoil, according to Bangou. Conflicts with Britain and Spain over the French colonies also contributed to the confusion. At the core of subsequent events, Bangou noted, were uprisings by slaves demanding the equal rights promised by the Revolution. These uprisings, along with France's need to raise armies to resist British efforts to take over her colonies, led to the effective end of slavery, which was officially declared by local administrators in Haiti and Guadeloupe in 1793. The following year, in 1794, the French National Assembly voted to confirm this local decision.

Between 1793 and 1802, Bangou asserted, the French colonies in the Caribbean lived through an unprecedented period of racial equality and prosperity.[8] Fighting alongside French troops and, in Haiti, led by black leaders, the former slaves demonstrated their capacity to organize their own societies. They had done this, he added, despite resistance from revolutionary leaders in Paris, who were not prepared to extend the promised equality and freedom to their colonies. The people of Guadeloupe and Haiti (Martinique was under English occupation during most of the Revolution) acted on their own behalf to take the freedom that had been promised. In the end, Bangou added, the French betrayed their Caribbean compatriots. In 1802, Napoleon Bonaparte decided to reestablish slavery. In Haiti, the French troops failed to overcome local resistance and the first black republic in the Americas was born. In Guadeloupe, despite heroic resistance on the part of black soldiers, slavery was reestablished.

The French Revolution, Bangou argued, deserved praise for promising freedom and equality to all. There were groups in France, most notably the Société des amis des noirs (the Society of Friends of the Blacks), that had actively sought the end of slavery even before 1789. But the opponents of slavery in France pursued immediate equality only for the mixed-race "free people of color," proposing a more gradual approach to freedom for the slaves. This divergent approach, he said, was rooted in the political need to appease colonial slave owners and, more importantly, in a belief that black slaves would be unable to adjust to immediate freedom.

In the discussion that followed Bangou's lecture, members of the audience were quick to draw parallels between the views of French revolutionaries in 1789 and their experiences in France in the 1980s. One commented that the impending inauguration of a single borderless European market, scheduled for the beginning of 1993, exhibited a similar betrayal of the people of the Antilles by the French. The single market would allow greater freedom for European goods and firms to exploit Martinique and Guadeloupe, but it did not provide resources and protection for Antilleans in their islands. Just as in 1789, he said, their concerns were left out of the political equation. Another audience member suggested that the failure of the Revolution to provide freedom in the Caribbean paralleled its eventual failure for the majority of French people. This comment was met with derision as someone pointed out that in France, nobody had been a slave before 1789 and nobody was forced back into slavery in 1802. The failure of the Revolution to make freedom for the slaves a priority was, one of the organizers said, in closing the discussion, one of the reasons why they had not sought to make the evening's event part of the official bicentennial commemorations.

IMMIGRATION:
FROM SOCIAL TO CULTURAL CHALLENGE

Watching the bicentennial parade a few months later, I was struck by the organizers' failure to include representations of the struggle against slavery in the French colonies. Antilleans I spoke with told me that they would not have expected the organizers to display the full ambiguity of that history, complete with French troops reinstating slavery. But a salute to Antillean revolutionary heroes, such as Toussaint Louverture and Louis Delgrès, would have helped reduce their own ambivalence regarding the bicentennial and would have gone a long way toward building their sense of inclusion in the life of the Republic. After all, the parade celebrated world cultural diversity, drawing on members of African and Arab immigrant communities in France to represent their countries of origin. Even as it celebrated diversity—and drew on the world to celebrate the French Revolution—the parade's design seemed to imply that France possessed a singularly coherent national culture, forged out of regional and class identities (Leruth 1998a; Dubois 2000). The contributions that France's large immigrant communities made to contemporary France did not seem to be part of this vision.

This was at odds with French history, since France has long been a country of immigrants. In the late nineteenth and early twentieth centuries, foreign workers formed the backbone of the French industrial working class. During the period between the two world wars, immigrant labor was actively recruited to meet the needs of French agriculture and business. In the 1920s, France had an immigration rate higher than that of the United States (Noiriel 1988, 21). It has been estimated that by 1931 over 3 million foreigners were living in France, constituting 7 percent of the total population. The majority of these migrants came from Poland, Italy, Spain, and Belgium; many also came from Greece, Czechoslovakia, Romania, Yugoslavia, and other Eastern European nations (Wihtol de Wenden 1988, 33, 37). Some of these immigrants returned to their home countries in the 1930s, but most settled in France. The famous image of Jean Gabin riding a locomotive in the bicentennial parade could easily have been that of an immigrant worker.

After World War II, French industry continued to rely on immigrant labor. Just as before the war, many immigrants were European, especially from Portugal, Spain, and Italy. However, many more arrived from North Africa, Turkey, southeast Asia, sub-Saharan Africa, and the Caribbean. The total numbers were about the same as in the 1930s, constituting 6–7 percent of the population of France (Kepel 1987; Noiriel 1988). As in previous periods, immigrants were concentrated in industrial work and agriculture. Even after a legal "suspension" of immigration was declared in 1974, policies that allowed family members to join immigrants already in France, ongoing immigration from other European Union member countries, political refugees seeking asylum, and illegal immigration contributed to maintaining the size of the immigrant population. France remains a country of immigration.

Historians claim that as many as a third of all French people have immigrant ancestors (Noiriel 1988, 10). Many well-known public figures, including some who are thought to represent the very essence of French identity—for example, entertainers Charles Aznavour (whose parents were Armenian) and Yves Montand (born in Italy)—are immigrants or are descended from immigrants. These facts are rarely made visible in representations of French national identity. Yet the subject of immigration is hardly hidden in France. Initially defined in both the interwar and postwar periods as *travailleurs étrangers* (foreign workers), susceptible to being sent back to their countries of origin when they were no longer needed, the integration of *immigrés* (immigrants), as they came to be known, has become central to public debates in France. Because they are no longer thought of as transitory migrants, the provision of housing, education, and jobs for these new settlers has become a major objective for social policy. The Third World and postcolonial origins of many postwar immigrants have also transformed public discussions of immigration. Race, ethnicity, and religion, most often glossed as cultural difference, while not entirely absent in the 1920s and 1930s, are now central to controversies surrounding immigration in France. The manner in which millions of immigrants can be assimilated into French culture—and the impact they will have on that culture—has become a fundamental question in French society.

THREE GIRLS ALMOST END THE REPUBLIC

In September 1989—two months after the bicentennial parade—Ernest Chenière, a middle school principal in Creil (a suburb of Paris), decided to expel three young girls from his school for wearing "Muslim scarves" (*foulard islamiques*) in class. By the middle of October, the affair of the Muslim scarves had become front-page news in national dailies and major news magazines and the subject of at least one debate in the National Assembly in which Minister of Education Lionel Jospin was obliged to take a stand. Jospin ultimately referred the affair to the Conseil d'Etat (a consultative body, often referred to for legal opinions) whose ambiguous ruling came down at the end of November. This did not settle the debate, which continues intermittently to this day (Beriss 1990; Feldblum 1999; Silverstein 2000).

The surprisingly intense controversy around this affair divided people in unusual ways. Usually supportive of the rights of immigrants, the political left was split, as people took positions that had more to do with the future form of French politics and identity than with their position in the political spectrum. The incident brought together people who had never been allied on immigration issues. Those opposed to religious symbols in the schools saw the *foulards* as a threat to the capability of the schools to educate and as a step toward unraveling the French Republic and national identity. Those not opposed saw the symbols as relatively unthreatening, an unfortunate habit from which Muslims could be weaned.

On one side were the secular republicans, who believed that all religious behavior should remain private. For this group, allowing children to wear symbols of their religious identity was a step toward educational chaos. It followed that if one group were allowed to bring its symbols into the schools, others would demand the same, spelling the end of tolerance. Each ethnic or religious community would then compete for control of the nation's schools, symbolizing, as one commentator put it, "the closing of each community against the others." Fears of ethnic "tribalism" and even civil war were cited.[9] Without these symbols all students would be equal individuals, their ethnic and religious differences rendered private.

Rhetoric rapidly escalated in the secular republican camp. In an open letter to the minister of education published in the weekly *Le Nouvel Observateur,* five prominent leftist intellectuals contended that it is "permitted to forbid" the wearing of scarves in the name of discipline. Their reference to and apparent repudiation of the slogan "it is forbidden to forbid" of the 1968 student uprisings in France, often associated with the authors of the letter, suggested that they did not see the wearing of scarves as a sign of individual freedom of expression. They argued that schools could not liberate students from narrow sectarian beliefs unless ethnic, religious, and political signs were barred. "To tolerate wearers of the Islamic scarf," they noted, "is not in any way liberating . . . [it] is instead simply opening the door to those who have decided once and for all to make the student bow down." The very foundation of French education was at stake, they argued, adding with considerable hyperbole that "the future will tell if the year of the Bicentennial will have also been that of the Munich of the Republican schools."[10]

On the other side of the debate were the "tolerant" republicans, led by the minister of education. His position was not that religious insignia should simply be allowed in schools. Rather, he argued a more fluid position in which the child's conscience would be respected while the basic elements of the educational system were upheld. Wearing scarves would be permitted, but proselytizing forbidden. Nobody would be excused from basic elements of educational programs, such as sex education or athletics, because of their beliefs. If parents rejected this position, he added, they were free to send their children to private schools. Some commentators argued that the rules concerning the separation of church and state meant that secular education should preserve the student's freedom from religious imposition from the teachers, not the other way around. Secular education, they noted, should be inherently tolerant of difference.[11] Others pointed out that there were far more flagrant signs of difference and inequality in the classroom already, such as the different clothing worn by rich and poor children.[12]

For proponents of tolerance, the danger in rejecting children for religious reasons resided in pushing them toward more extreme positions. Immigrants—including Muslims—can be integrated into the French Republic, they insisted, but not through rejection. One article pointed out that the "community reflex" had become important among Muslims precisely because their religion had been mistreated in the press and by French society as a whole. The best way to teach equality and tolerance, in their view, was to expose children to other ways of living in school. Yet even this more tolerant camp assumed that such exposure would inevitably lead students, especially young women, to abandon their ties to Islam. One commentator wrote that in the public schools scarf-wearing girls would learn to develop their own independent identities, "in other words, they will remove the veil."[13] Education Minister Jospin claimed that the schools, if they accepted these students, would be freeing them from the isolation of their families and providing them with the intellectual tools necessary for their liberation.[14]

At the end of November, the Conseil d'Etat ruled that it would be legal to wear the scarves but illegal to proselytize in the schools. The ruling did little to end the debate. During the following decade, successive governments tried various strategies to limit the representation of religious and ethnic identities in the schools. While some analysts argued from the beginning that tolerance of visible signs of difference was required in a society that was becoming increasingly multiethnic, most political leaders and pundits insisted—and continue to insist—that the main objective of policy should be to prevent the development of ethnic communities in France.[15]

A number of issues were raised by the Islamic scarf affair. The ability of the French state to maintain a secular public school system and, by extension, the secular nature of French political life was seen by many to be the central issue in the affair. After all, the French public school system was initially designed to help establish the legitimacy of the secular republic against the resistance of the Catholic Church. However, despite the significant growth of Islam in France in recent decades, Muslims still represent a small minority, especially when compared to the near universality of Catholicism in late-nineteenth-century France, when the school system was created. An oft-repeated joke in the early 1990s suggested that if Islam had become the second-largest religion in France, fear of Islam had become the first. Yet if three little girls in scarves were not a serious threat to secularity, why the enormous controversy?

The bicentennial celebrations displayed an idea of a French national culture undivided by ethnicity or religion. In the Bastille Day parade, France seemed to celebrate the diversity of world cultures. But as Antillean reactions to those events suggested, one legacy of the Revolution was the unequal manner in which representatives of those diverse cultures were integrated into French society. The scarf affair served to sharpen the debate around France's capacity to integrate "Third World immigrants." How could these postwar immigrants and their children become French? Were they too culturally different to integrate into French society? Would they form distinct ethnic communities, leading to American-style ghettos and ethnic politics in France? Could France be multicultural and remain true to its revolutionary heritage? Despite the public discussion of "cultural difference," was "race" likely to become a central social division? These questions, raised by the bicentennial celebrations and the scarf affair, became the central themes of public debate in France in the following decade.

THE CULTURE OF FRENCH *CULTURE*

In the 1990s, fear of developing ethnic identities in France, as manifested by scarf-wearing girls in public schools, helped launch a national debate about the meaning of being French. Both the intensity and the content of this debate are related to the way in which the idea of the French nation has formed since the end of the nineteenth century. Although the groups involved in recent conflicts over ethnicity may be new, the terms of the debate have not changed significantly. One reason that the rise of public ethnicity is problematic is precisely because it recalls conflicts that have marked the development of politics in France. The dominant ideas of what constitutes French national culture were formed through these debates during the past century.

At least two versions of French cultural identity competed for dominance in the late nineteenth and early twentieth centuries, and both continue to play significant roles in struggles over French identity today. The more well known of these cultural ideologies is that of republican universalism, in which adherence to the nation is defined explicitly as a choice. Ernest Renan made this point when he suggested the nation can be summed up as "a palpable fact: based on consent, it is the clearly expressed desire to live in a community. The existence of a nation is . . . a daily plebiscite" (1992, 55). Renan (1992, 46) argued that France was a mixture of many races, thus eliminating the possibility of a pure French race. To make the nation out of the fusion of diverse peoples, there had to be a combination of common memories, which could be achieved through either actual experience or education and mutual consent (Noiriel 1988, 28; cf. Todorov 1989, 256, 257; Birnbaum 1993, 38; Said 1978). Such ideas are not uncommon in France today. Arguing for a France without ethnic specificities, the philosopher Alain Finkielkraut has written that "a nation to which one can be attached in heart and mind is a nation that is organized as a gathering of individuals, united by a conscious and rational adherence to certain principles, principles such as those contained in the expression 'France, land of the rights of Man'" (Espaces 1985, 41; Balibar 1991, 24; Wieviorka 1997; Leruth 1998b).

These ideas about the nation were not only reflected in philosophical discussions but also became part of social science discourse. Historian Gérard Noiriel has suggested that it is possible to link some of the ideas held by turn-of-the-century French sociologists, such as Emile Durkheim and Marcel Mauss, to Renan's ideas about the nation. While these social scientists generally avoided addressing overtly political issues in their research, Noiriel (1998, 32–33) argues that, given the intensity of anti-Semitism manifest in political debates in late-nineteenth- and early-twentieth-century France, it was in their interest as French Jews to argue that notions of racial determinism, or even of a common history, had little influence on members of a modern society. In his *Division of Labor in Society* (1947), for instance, Durkheim asserted the idea that modern society is characterized by "organic solidarity." In this view, the individual is attached to society not through a particular race, family, or tradition but through a specialized role in society. Furthermore, Durkheim stressed the importance of formal institutions, such as schools, in forming the individual. In a similar vein, Mauss (1969, 588) argued that a nation cannot exist until all groups that might divide an individual's loyalty to the state have been eliminated. A nation, for Mauss (1969, 593), is characterized by a population that has been homogenized by national institutions, not one that is homogeneous because of anterior characteristics such as race.

The idea of a French people homogenized through education in the values of the Republic can be contrasted with another influential version of French national identity based on ideas about history, tradition, and religion. Culture is also central to this "closed nationalism," but the sources of this culture are not those of the French Revolution and republican ideology (Winock 1990). Although various monarchist, Bonapartist, and Catholic groups resisted the development of a republican state throughout the nineteenth century, the defeat of France by Germany in 1871 and the establishment of the Third Republic a few years later provided the basis for the development of a conservative vision of "true France" that would operate (mostly) within the boundaries set by the republican order (Lebovics 1992). In this view the nation could be understood as a combination of territory and history, as the nationalist politician and writer Maurice Barrès put it, of the land and the dead (Todorov 1989, 257). This contrasted with a portrayal of modern, urban, industrial France as corrupt and cosmopolitan. Real France, from this perspective, still existed among supporters of regionalist identities who resisted the authority of the centralized state and among peasants (see Rogers 1987; Lehning 1995).

This view of a distinction between the "legal" nation (the Republic) and the "real" nation, based on regional history and peasant traditions, was promoted by Catholic nationalists and others at the turn of the century and has been central to the ideologies of various movements since then, including Jean-Marie Le Pen's National Front (Hazareesingh 1994, 130). This version of French national identity portrays France as profoundly Catholic, against the secular republican state, but also against the presence of Jews, Protestants, and, in the postwar era, Muslims (Birnbaum 1993, 295). This "national-Catholicism," as historian Pierre Birnbaum (1993, 298) has called it, is most often associated with the extreme right. Yet attributing this view only to the right in France would be a mistake, since the idea of an eternal France, rooted in the soil and tradition, has also served the left at various times (Winock 1990; Rogers 1987). The study of French folklore, for instance, although rooted in conservative traditions that emphasize "blood and history," was institutionalized under the progressive Popular Front in 1937—with the establishment of the Musée National des Arts et Traditions Populaires (ATP)—but was subsequently used by both right- and left-wing governments (Chiva 1987; Lebovics 1992).

These different ideas of France as a unified culture, joining the people of France in a common territory, language, and history, rose to prominence at a time (the end of the nineteenth century) when the model of a secular republic was being contested and when, furthermore, many of the people living in what is now France did not necessarily think of themselves as French. Such ideas replaced local conceptions of identity with broader, national terms. However, claiming authority for a republic based on a sovereign people required the creation of a French people who would recognize themselves as sovereign, rather than accept the authority of monarchies legitimized by claims of blood or the alternative legitimacy of the Church. In the dominant model for French identity that resulted from this period, the central element that defines a member of French society is his or her relationship to the state. This relationship provides the basic symbolic framework for defining what is, and is not, French. The territory governed by the state is defined as one culturally uniform space in which the citizens act to produce the general interest of the nation, not as representatives of subcultures or races, but as members of French culture. The legitimacy of the state rests on its ability to represent this putatively homogeneous cultural community.

In the context of debates about postwar immigration, questions about how to define French identity remain central. One powerful set of ideas draws on a notion of culture in which being French is something one can learn, so that immigrants and colonial populations can be made French, just as peasants supposedly were in the past. People—including immigrants—are understood to become French, in this view, as individuals, through a process of abandoning attachment to other cultures or at least making that attachment private and inconsequential for participation in the political life of the nation. Although this idea of national identity is "open" in the sense that people can become French, it is quite different from American ideas of tolerant "multiculturalism," where ties to subcultural groups are respected and celebrated. Such groups have no place in this view of French identity.

An idea of French culture rooted in territory, history, and religion also plays a role in defining French identity. Long associated with the antirepublican right, this "closed" version of French identity views culture as inherited from the past, created out of regional histories and long association with Catholicism. Culture is a form of wealth (*patrimoine*) that has been accumulated over the centuries, resulting in the French nation. As I have noted, concern for this French cultural "heritage" is hardly confined to the right. It is the object of study by social scientists, representation in ethnographic museums and parks around the country, preservation through government agencies, and annual celebration in national *journées du patrimoine* (Cultural Heritage Days). This view of identity contrasts sharply with a view in which culture is something one may simply join at will. To be French, as Sartre (1954, 57) pointed out, is to understand implicitly the significance of the objects and ideas that make up the national cultural wealth. According to proponents of this point of view, Antilleans and other immigrants are simply incapable of understanding or contributing to this national wealth.

CULTURE AS RACE

The dominant ideology in France defines the nation as one unified culture, rather than a collection of subcultures. In theory, immigrants can become French, but they must abandon any public attachment to their cultures of origin. To insist on maintaining those cultures or, worse, to demand recognition of their cultural distinctiveness from the French state threatens the cultural unity of the nation. Part of the controversy surrounding immigration in the 1990s was based on the perception that postwar immigrants were doing just that. At the same time, it is not clear that French policymakers and cultural critics actually believe that many of the non-European immigrants and their descendants currently in France are capable of abandoning their cultures of origin and becoming French. Adopting what has been called a "cultural fundamentalist" position, these immigrants are viewed as being trapped in their cultures of origin (Stolcke 1995). In this view, culture—including French national *culture*—comes to resemble the race concept used in the United States.

For many people in France, the legacy of "scientific" racism in the twentieth century, the Nazis, and American segregation has served to discredit any public attempts to divide humanity into a racial hierarchy. French social scientists have been known to express shock when they discover that scholarship by their American colleagues often deals very directly with the subject (Ghasarian 1994). In fact, the idea of a distinctly cultural identity for the French nation was in part formed against notions of biologically determined race. Many of the racial theories developed by French thinkers in the nineteenth century were more warmly received in Britain, Germany, and the United States than in France (Mosse 1978, 57). Some theorists, such as Renan, who had developed ideas about the racial heritage of the French in mid-century, later abandoned those ideas in favor of more open notions of French identity (Birnbaum 1993). Since the late nineteenth century, citizenship laws in France have been framed around the idea of assimilation, rather than the racial ideologies that have framed those laws in other countries (Brubaker 1992, chap. 5; Feldblum 1999).

Although prominent French scientists were involved in the eugenics movement in the early twentieth century, their impact on policy and ideas about French identity were nearly imperceptible (Taguieff 1994; Schneider 1990, 1994). By the 1920s, promoters of racial ideas in French social science were marginalized when students of Durkheim's school of sociology rose to prominence in French universities and politics (Lebovics 1992, 34). The failure of racial ideologies to become part of dominant views of French national identity also can be attributed to concerns with solidifying the legitimacy of the Republic and, in the early twentieth century, with ensuring the growth of the population. France's loss to Germany in 1871 and the slaughter of World War I, combined with other factors such as the Catholic Church's opposition to birth control, rendered illegitimate efforts to focus on putative racial purity (Taguieff 1994, 88, 94).

Although explicit racial ideologies lack legitimacy in France, color often serves as a marker of difference from a putative French ideal. In addition, racism clearly exists in France, as I outlined in Chapter 1. Antilleans in France often complain that "French people cannot tell an Antillean from an African."

Color is one term in a complex ideology defining belonging and foreignness in France that focuses primarily on culture. For instance, racism in France is not principally defined by attention to color or by the deployment of racial stereotypes (although it can be). Instead, racism is understood primarily as an incorrect or unjust invocation of culture.

A variety of discourses, state administrations, and rituals operate in France to reduce religious, regional, and linguistic diversity to manageable aspects of a culturally homogeneous whole. The discourses that control the development of alternative sites for public identity in French society not only frame the cultural inside, defining those traits that make someone French, but also ascribe characteristics to those who are outside. The cultural inside is characterized by diversity, but that diversity is contained through carefully orchestrated state mechanisms, as well as through clear definitions of public and private domains. Those who are on the outside belong not only in different cultures, but in cultures that are qualitatively different. It is the invocation of such cultural differences that can lead to accusations of racism, but, ironically, it is also through their invocation that such accusations can be denied. Drawing a line between a respectful and a racist invocation of cultural difference can be difficult.

For Americans, many of the representations of black people current in French society provoke discomfort, since they often seem to reproduce the racial stereotyping that is condemned in the United States. Over the course of my fieldwork, I was often surprised by representations of black people that I imagined would be unthinkable in the United States. For instance, one trendy journal, *L'Echo des savanes*, carried a serious article concerning the position of black people in France that featured a suggestively posed nude black woman on its cover, smeared with caviar.[16] In a television advertisement, a scrawny white man was shown in a track meet with several athletic-looking black men. The white man appeared to have no hope of winning, until he ate the advertised candy, turned black, and won the race. A billboard advertisement for the *Cosby Show* featured a large photo of a laughing Bill Cosby. The advertisement read, "On M6, the 8:00 P.M. news presenter is black, and he isn't even a news presenter," thus (theoretically) startling the French viewer with the idea that the anchor could be black, then startling the viewer even more with the idea that the channel would dare to broadcast something other than the news at 8:00 P.M. (see Fig. 2.1). Sex, sports, and farce, among the key elements in racist stereotypes of people of African origin, are all reproduced in these and many other situations in France.

While I was surprised by these images, I was shocked by the relative indifference such representations evoked among Antilleans I knew. The racial stereotypes that frequently appeared in the mass media, I was often told, were ridiculous but not worth getting upset about. Because they depicted "generic" black people, they were not really about Antilleans anyhow. This indifference

Figure 2.1   The *Cosby Show* in France, an alternative to the news hour.

was evident, for instance, in reactions to a Canadian film, provocatively entitled *Comment faire l'amour avec un nègre sans se fatiguer* (How to make love to a Negro without getting tired), depicting the amorous adventures of two black men with white women in Montreal that I viewed with Antillean friends in 1989 (see Fig. 2.2). While they criticized the film's story, they were not terribly concerned with its depiction of race relations, pointing out that it was about people in Montreal, not Paris. Antilleans, much like the critics in French newspapers, objected to the film's failure to identify the origins of the black protagonists. Without an idea of the cultural origins of the characters, they told me, it was difficult to make sense of their motivations.[17] While stereotypical representations of black people in France may provoke discomfort, it is because such representations are out of place in a society where difference is primarily understood as cultural. Thus one does not speak of race relations and there is no French social scientific literature devoted to that topic. Groups are most often identified in national cultural terms.

This division of the world according to cultures rather than races has long been evident in French social science and corresponds in many ways with the management of cultural diversity in France. Countries colonized by France were the objects of study, providing an ideological counter to the type of society that was being created in France at the turn of the century. This is particularly evident in the distinctions that Durkheim drew between France as a modern collectivity of individuals and other societies, defined by "mechanical

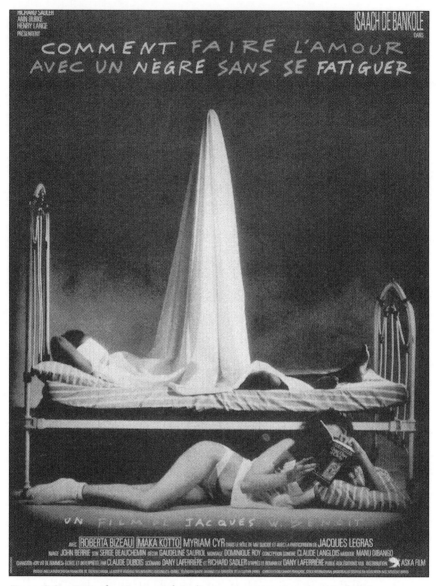

Figure 2.2   Poster for *Comment faire l'amour avec un nègre sans se fatiguer.*

solidarity" (Durkheim 1947; Noiriel 1988). Such societies were understood to be largely homogeneous and frozen in time. At least implicitly (and often explicitly), European society was placed at the higher end of an evolutionary scale, described as exhibiting organic solidarity and thus a good deal of variety in ideas and behavior, while other societies were characterized by monotonous repetition of the same forms and structures. These societies could be studied in order to view traits of European societies in their pristine, premodern state, as Durkheim argued in *Elementary Forms of the Religious Life* (1965).

French social science continues to emphasize the distinctions between simple, generally non-European societies and complex, "advanced" Western societies (Balibar 1991). This is evident in the choices made by French anthropologists to study, for instance, Amazonian Indians rather than urban Brazilians or Venezuelans. It is evident as well in the efforts of anthropologists who choose to work in France and focus on the kinship practices of peasants and especially the documentation of practices that are fast disappearing, rather than on contemporary social change. In much of this contemporary work, the structural distinctions between societies drawn by Durkheim are transformed into cultural distinctions, framing the manner in which members of particular societies understand the world. Thus, for instance, Louis Dumont (1986) has written about the contrasts between the individualist "modern" ideology found in complex societies and the holistic ideology, or culture, of what he calls "traditional" societies. One of the results of this perspective is a notion of the non-European members of traditional societies as especially distant in cultural terms, being unable to think or act outside of the all-encompassing ideas of their society.

In France, this totalizing view of non-European (supposedly non- or premodern) cultures is not limited to the realm of social science. It pervades popular culture through film and advertising, as well as ideological debates. Everyone seems to be an expert, as Michel Panoff (1986, 325) has noted, basing their knowledge on trips to exotic places or television documentaries. Furthermore, no member of a third world nation is exempt from the exoticizing treatment. Thus, in an interview concerning events in South Africa, the evening news anchor asked President Mobutu of Zaire if he traveled everywhere with his "fetish cane." An advertisement for a series of multicultural concerts carried a photo of the South African musician Miriam Makeba. Below it were a few phrases, scribbled as if by the hand of a poetic music critic: "Could it be that all that is beautiful in Africa is run through with violence?" In the late 1980s and early 1990s, a weekly television program called *Latitudes* presented news and features from France's overseas departments and territories, each week including one segment devoted to a documentary about the cultures of these diverse places. More often than not, these documentaries focused on the rituals and cultures of the exotic South Pacific, especially on the peoples of Wallis and Futuna or, failing that, on the Kanaks of New Caledonia. Segments devoted to the non-Kanak majority of the population or the fishermen of St. Pierre and Miquelon, two French islands off the east coast of Canada, were rare.

From this point of view, the world is populated by people who belong to discrete cultures rather than races. These cultures are not, however, represented as equivalent. While French culture enables the nation, culture outside of Europe renders people incapable of critical thinking and prevents them from developing those qualities the French deem essential to their own identity, such as individualism (Herzfeld 1987, 36). This idea of the culture of others allows some French leaders to argue that immigrants—even scarf-wearing little girls who have probably never lived anywhere but France—belong inescapably to cultures whose values are incompatible with those of the Republic.

As I have noted, accusations of racism in France are most often based on perceptions of the unjust invocation of cultural difference. Thus French municipal leaders have been accused of racism for justifying exclusion of immigrants from public housing on the basis of a "threshold of tolerance," a percentage of foreigners in a building's population beyond which French people would be driven out. They argue that there is a measurable point beyond which cultures simply cannot be mixed and often point to Lebanon, the former Yugoslavia, or the United States as examples of failed attempts to make such mixtures work. Such views are understood to be racist because they invoke culture in order to justify discrimination. This view appears, as Etienne Balibar has remarked, as a "racism without races . . . a racism which, at first sight, does not postulate the superiority of certain groups or peoples in relation to others but 'only' the harmfulness of abolishing frontiers, the incompatibility of life-styles and traditions" (1991, 21).[18]

Social Disorder and the Republic of Soccer

The ideals of republican universalism hold out the promise of integration to immigrants in France, no matter what their origin. For postwar immigrants of color, however, that promise of integration is limited by cultural fundamentalism and racism. They are understood to come from cultures that are qualitatively different from the cultures of European immigrants, cultures that they cannot abandon. Even the children of immigrants who have always lived in France are thought of as belonging to their parents' culture of origin and lacking the ability to assimilate into French society. This is not simply a racial argument. Similar claims were made in the 1930s about southern and eastern European immigrants, who were thought to be too culturally different to assimilate into French society (Wihtol de Wenden 1991). In representations of national values, such as the bicentennial parade, French society is displayed as a beacon that may inspire people from other cultures, but not as a society they might join. Even Jessye Norman, singing the French national anthem while wrapped in the flag, represents "the world's ghetto mothers," not France itself. The ghetto mothers presumably live somewhere else.

During the 1990s, immigrants were increasingly represented in France as a source of social disorder. In the view of many, the failure of schools to make French citizens out of immigrant children, as indexed by the persistence of scarf wearing among girls, became the failure of schools to educate and civi-lize. A perceived rise in violence in schools—attacks on teachers, mugging of students, for instance—was often blamed on immigrant children, who were thought to be forming gangs, following an American model widely under-stood as pernicious. Outside of schools, rising crime rates, especially in public transportation, the spread of graffiti, periodic riots in public housing com-plexes, and rumors of neighborhoods in the working-class suburbs that police were afraid to enter were also attributed to immigrants. The association be-tween immigrants and social disorder culminated in efforts to address the problem of illegal immigration, the *sans papiers* (undocumented immigrants), whose very existence associated immigration with illegality (Rosello 1998).

The growing association between immigration and social disorder was paralleled by the development of the idea that immigrants, especially Mus-lims, were organizing to undermine the foundations of the Republic. During the initial scarf affair in 1989 some journalists and policymakers had warned that scarf-wearing girls were the avant-garde for a Muslim invasion designed to turn the French republic into the next Iran. The idea of a Muslim conspir-acy grew after the start of an especially bloody civil war in Algeria in 1992. Terrorist incidents in France related to that war gave rise to the idea that en-tire terrorist networks were implanted there, supported by the North African community. Scholars and journalists began to track the putative influence of Islamic organizations linked to terrorism among immigrant youth.

These mirror negative images of immigrants in French—as the seeds of social disorder and the organized elements of a potential uprising—repeated some of the same stereotypes used in the nineteenth century to describe the developing French working class (Chevalier 1973). Just as in earlier periods, the sense that society was spiraling out of control contributed to the rise of calls for law and order and to the success of xenophobic political parties, such as the National Front, that promised to provide that order. By the mid-1990s, the sense of crisis in France was palpable. Even plans in 1996 to commemo-rate the fifteen hundredth anniversary of the Catholic conversion of the Frankish king Clovis were swept up in the debates around social disorder and immigration (Terrio 1999). The sense that the Republic was reaching a break-ing point was best illustrated in a film directed by Mathieu Kassovitz entitled *Hate* (1995). The movie portrayed three young working-class men, one of Arab origin, another African, and the third Jewish, as they wandered about their riot-wrecked housing development in a Paris suburb, contemplating re-venge on the police for killing a friend. A story is repeated through the movie about a man who falls from a high floor in a skyscraper. As he passes each floor he says to himself, "So far, so good." But just as he is hurtling toward in-evitable disaster, the film portrays France itself, spinning toward destruction.

In 1998, the largest sporting event in the world, the World Cup of soccer, came to France and, for a moment at least, seemed to change the sense of inevitable disaster. The World Cup, like the bicentennial nearly a decade earlier, provided the French government with an opportunity to represent French identity to the world. Having failed to qualify for the previous two World Cups, in 1990 and 1994, the French national team (as host, it qualified automatically in 1998) inspired low expectations. I arrived in France in late June, when the competition had already begun, but found little more than cynical interest among my metropolitan French and Antillean friends. Nearly everyone I initially spoke with seemed to think that the cup was an overly commercialized spectacle of interest mostly to sportswear promoters. They condemned the violence associated with soccer fans, the nationalist overtones of the game, and the expense of building new stadiums, especially the enormous Stade de France, constructed in the working-class and immigrant Parisian suburb of St. Denis. The government seemed more willing to invest in entertainment for the masses than help develop jobs or improve education. Putting the main event stadium in St. Denis, a town where economic investment of another sort seemed called for, was seen as especially insensitive. Initial coverage of the event in France focused on disappointingly high hotel vacancies, ticket distribution scandals, and the violent acts committed by hooligans from Germany.

Interest in the cup began to shift, however, with France's June 28 victory against Paraguay and especially its overtime victory on July 3 against longtime rival Italy, which put the French team into the semifinals. The semifinal game against Croatia drew huge audiences around the country, with over a third of the population watching the match on television (Markovits 1998, 12). In the Paris neighborhood where I was staying, restaurants and cafés were overflowing with crowds gathered around television sets; millions of others watched at home. France's victory set off massive street celebrations throughout the country that were only rivaled in size by France's defeat of Brazil in the cup final on July 12. As many as 2 million people celebrated the French victories in the streets of Paris that evening and the following day, crowding the Champs-Elysées with a sea of people that was compared by some with the celebrations that followed the liberation of Paris from Nazi occupation in 1944. A few days later, an estimated 500,000 people took to the streets for Bastille Day festivities, nearly twice the number of the previous year (Markovits 1998, 11–12).

Although a World Cup victory would be cause for celebration in nearly any country with a soccer-playing tradition, the French victory seemed to indicate a renewed sense of national unity. Immigration and immigrants were at the center of this victory. The diverse origins of the national team players—Senegal, Ghana, Algeria, Guadeloupe, Martinique, French Guiana, New Caledonia, and Armenia, as well as metropolitan France—were cited as evidence that diversity could contribute to national glory. In addition to being immigrants or children of immigrants, several of the players had grown up in the same putatively tough working-class suburbs that many thought were the source of crime and disorder. Lilian Thuram, born in Guadeloupe and raised in the suburbs of Paris, scored the two decisive goals in France's match against Croatia; Zinedine Zidane, son of Algerian immigrants from the suburbs of Marseille, scored the winning goals against Brazil in the cup final. The crowds on the Champs-Elysées shouted "Zidane for president!" and immense pictures of "Zizou" and the other team members were projected on one of the fundamental symbols of the French nation, the Arc de Triomphe (see Fig. 2.3).

The diversity of the team was matched by the diversity of the crowds celebrating their victory. The Champs-Elysées was crowded with millions of people, including many who had come into the city from the suburbs. Faces painted in the blue, white, and red French national colors, wearing blue team jerseys, and waving the French flag, suburban youth mixed with middle- and upper-class white Parisians. The masses of supposedly poorly integrated immigrant youth suddenly appeared to be deeply attached to their French identity. Playing on the diversity of the suburbs, commentators noted that the celebration of the "blue, white, and red" had become a celebration of the "black, white, and *beur*" (*beur* is a slang term for Arab).[19] One columnist wrote that after the celebrations, "a now-black, white, and beur France . . . went to bed exhausted, happy, and reconciled with its true nature."[20]

Figure 2.3   France 1998 World Cup Team. AP/WIDE WORLD PHOTOS.

The World Cup victory was seen as a victory for France as a whole and for immigrants in particular. The team's diversity was understood as a slap in the face to the leaders of the xenophobic right-wing parties. Jean-Marie Le Pen, leader of the National Front, had dismissed the team months earlier as not truly French. Its victory and the ensuing massive celebrations suggested that he was out of step with France. In addition, the massive stadium in St. Denis was now seen as just the right kind of infrastructure for the suburbs, likely to contribute to the development of jobs for immigrant youth.[21] An adviser to the interior minister was quoted as saying that Zidane's moves on the field had done more than a decade of integration policies in making immigrants feel French.[22]

Sports, in general, and soccer, in particular, have long served as a means for social mobility and cultural integration for immigrants in France (Noiriel 1988, 320). But the 1998 World Cup team was seen by many as symbolizing something more than integration. It stood for a newly multicultural France and a model of multiculturalism that somehow included the "genius" of the French republican model of society, as distinct from the American model that emphasized distinct ethnic communities. Sociologist Edgar Morin noted that soccer, like a nation, requires individual heroism and team cohesion. He claimed that the World Cup team displayed these qualities and, in their victory, transmitted them to the entire population, creating a moment of national ecstasy and togetherness.[23] Others were more suspicious of the claim that France was becoming multicultural. For all their putative diversity, the players won as members of the French national team, wearing national colors and symbols. Philosopher Alain Finkielkraut warned against multicultural conclusions, arguing that the integration of immigrants still required individual adhesion to a national culture.[24]

WHAT PRICE FRENCHNESS?

The French victory in the World Cup produced a moment of national euphoria. The conflicts of the preceding decade seemed vanquished by the multicultural team and the equally multicultural crowds waving the French flag in the streets. Charles Pasqua, a former minister of the interior known for his hard-line position on illegal immigration, called for the government to take immediate steps to issue legal residency permits to the *sans papiers*. Antillean fans I knew had initially supported the Brazilian team, but they had been drawn into the national celebration by the crucial role of Guadeloupan and Martinican players in the French victory. Like the slaves-turned-soldiers in 1789, the Antilleans and other immigrants on the French national team proved that they too were worthy of equality in France.

However, the national euphoria did not last long. Fear of crime and the rise of "social exclusion" in the immigrant and working-class suburbs soon returned to the center of French political debates. Candidates of the right and left ran for office promising to address the problem of "insecurity," which had become a code word for immigration. In 2002, the far right anti-immigrant leader Jean-Marie Le Pen came in second in the first round of the presidential elections and found himself in a runoff with the incumbent, Gaullist Jacques Chirac. Political commentators were quick to point out that the electorate was deeply divided, so that Le Pen had won—beating, most notably, the socialist leader, who had been expected to face Chirac in the runoff—without earning many more votes than in past elections. However, his victory suggested that substantial anti-immigrant sentiment still existed in France. After massive street demonstrations throughout France called on voters to defeat Le Pen in the second round, Chirac was reelected with a lopsided 82 percent of the vote. But the clash of symbols, between the apparent integration of immigrants into a new multicultural France and their equally apparent rejection continued—and continues—unresolved.

The promise of equality as citizens of France, held out to Antilleans on and off since 1789, is at the core of this conflict. Theoretically Antilleans and other immigrants can enjoy equality if they are willing to make their own cultural traditions and values private and join French society as individuals. In reality, the price of becoming French may be impossibly high. While the "open" strand of French national ideology appears to welcome the adherence of individuals to the nation, the "closed" strand promotes a view that the gap between French and foreign cultures, especially the "third world" immigrants and their children currently in France, as too wide to be bridged. Even the bicentennial celebration of the "planet's tribes" situated those tribes outside of France.

The problem faced by Antilleans, with their long association with France, is slightly different. For them, the price of Frenchness appeared in 1989 to require that they forget the history of the Antilles during the 1789 Revolution in favor of a standardized French celebration of that period. Yet for many Antilleans, the betrayal of the promise of equality by the French revolutionaries in 1789 and the reenslavement of their ancestors in 1802 are the template on which their relations with France have been built over the past two centuries. The question of whether French people and policymakers saw Antilleans as equals was especially evident in the organization of Antillean migration, starting in the 1960s. They were also manifest in the efforts to commemorate the 150th anniversary of the definitive end of slavery in the French colonies, in 1998, that are the subject of the next chapter.

Notes

1. See Dubois 2000; Lcruth 1998a; Kaplan 1995; and Northcutt 1991 for other analyses of the bicentennial celebrations.

2. Serge July, *Libération*, July 15–16, 1989.

3. Jean Hatzfeld, *Libération*, July 15–16, 1989.

4. Hatzfeld, *Libération*, July 15–16, 1989.

5. Eric Dupin, *Libération*, July 14, 1989. See Kaplan 1995 for an examination of some of the objections to the bicentennial celebrations.

6. For additional insights into this period and its implications for more recent French policies, see Dubois 1999, 2000; Dorigny 1995; Kadish 2000.

7. Triangular trade refers to the importation of slaves to European colonies in the Americas that was paid for through the exportation of goods from those colonies to Europe.

8. This is a controversial assertion; cf. Dubois 1999.

9. Jacques Julliard, *Le Nouvel Observateur*, October 26–November 1, 1989.

10. *Le Nouvel Observateur*, November 2–8, 1989. The reference is to the French and British appeasement of Hitler in Munich in 1938.

11. Guy Sitbon, *Le Nouvel Observateur*, November 9–15, 1989; Jean Daniel, *Le Nouvel Observateur*, November 2–8, 1989.

12. Harlem Désir, *Le Nouvel Observateur*, November 9–15, 1989.

13. Claude Allègre, *Le Nouvel Observateur*, November 9–15, 1989.

14. *Le Nouvel Observateur*, October 26–November 1, 1989.

15. Early advocates of a multiculturalist position included anthropologist Marc Augé and editor of the daily *Libération*, Serge July. See *Libération*, November 20, 1989, 13; *Libération*, October 23, 1989, 3. The dominant positions developed in 1989 were mostly unchanged in discussions of a project to make wearing religious insignia illegal in schools in 2003. See *Le Monde*, June 18, 2003.

16. *L'Echo des Savanes* 70 (1989).

17. See *Le Monde*, August 26, 1989, for a French review and the *Village Voice*, June 6, 1990, for a very different American perspective.

18. See also Guillaumin 1981. Paul Gilroy (1987, 1990) provides a similar perspective on the transformation of the concepts of race, nation, and culture in Britain.

19. Edgar Morin, "La victoire miraculeuse a fait surgir ce qui était à la fois très profond et invisible: Les fondements mystiques et mythiques de l'appartenance nationale. Une extase historique," *Libération*, July 20, 1998.

20. Alain Lipietz, "La fête du 12 juillet est la rencontre magique du courant né en décembre 1995 et d'un symbole adéquat: l'équipe d'Aimé Jacquet. Le Carnaval social," *Libération*, July 29, 1998.

21. Dominique Sanchez, "La banlieue, l'autre vainqueur du Mondial," *Le Monde*, July 24, 1998. See also Silverstein 2000 for an analysis of sports and social policy directed toward immigrants in France.

22. Renaud Dely, "Zidane, icône de l'intégration. Il est présenté comme un symbole de réussite," *Libération*, July 10, 1998.

23. Morin, "La victoire miraculeuse."

24. Alain Finkielkraut, "Vanité française," *Le Monde*, July 21, 1998.

Further Reading

Birnbaum, Pierre. 2001. *The Idea of France.* Translated by M. B. DeBevoise. New York: Hill & Wang. A historical analysis of the central debates between closed and open versions of French national identity.

Brubaker, Rogers. 1992. *Citizenship and Nationhood in France and Germany.* Cambridge: Harvard University Press. A comparative history of citizenship policies and their relationship to France's and Germany's distinctive ways of defining what it means to belong in each society, this book raises questions about the dominant models used in thinking about national identity around the world.

Cole, Jeffrey. 1997. *The New Racism in Europe: A Sicilian Ethnography.* Cambridge: Cambridge University Press. An ethnographic study of the conflicts surrounding immigration in southern Italy that focuses on how the receiving society determines the meaning of immigration.

Feldblum, Miriam. 1999. *Reconstructing Citizenship: The Politics of Nationality Reform and Immigration in Contemporary France.* Albany: SUNY Press. This analysis places debates about immigration and citizenship policy in France in their proper historical context.

Hargreaves, Alec G. 1995. *Immigration, "Race," and Ethnicity in Contemporary France.* London: Routledge. In this broad survey of immigration in France in the latter half of the twentieth century, Hargreaves provides useful insights into immigrant activism and French public policy.

Noiriel, Gérard. 1996. *The French Melting Pot: Immigration, Citizenship, and National Identity.* Translated by Geoffroy de Laforcade. Minneapolis: University of Minnesota Press. In this critical history of immigration in France, Noiriel connects the actual story of immigration with the making of the ideas that are central to French identity.

CHAPTER THREE

BETRAYED ANTILLES, BROKEN FRENCH PROMISES

A Duty to Remember

In the winter of 1987, I participated in a seminar at the Ecole des Hautes Etudes en Sciences Sociales in Paris with an interdisciplinary group of anthropologists and historians. One day we found ourselves discussing the revolutions of 1848 in Europe. As we went around the table, some of the scholars made remarks concerning the significance of the events of that year. As a graduate student, I was fortunate to have permission to attend the seminar, and I hesitated to speak. Nevertheless, I raised my hand and pointed out that in 1848 the French government definitively abolished slavery in its colonies. There was a moment of silence. A historian, a well-known scholar of nineteenth-century France, turned toward me and said in a dismissive tone, "That was more a problem for the Americas than for Europe."

In 1998, the French government organized the commemoration of the 150th anniversary of the abolition of slavery in the colonies. Although celebrated on a much smaller scale than the 1989 bicentennial of the French Revolution, dozens of events in both metropolitan France and the overseas departments marked this anniversary. The minister of culture and communications, Catherine Trautmann, announced the themes of the government-sponsored events at an inaugural press conference in early April, declaring the year would be devoted to a celebration of human rights. Along with the sesquicentennial of the abolition of slavery, she remarked, 1998 was also the 400th anniversary of the Edict of Nantes, granting religious freedom to Protestants in France, the centennial of the publication of Emile Zola's manifesto *J'accuse* (I accuse) denouncing the anti-Semitic persecution of Captain Alfred Dreyfus, and the fiftieth anniversary of the U.N. adoption of the Universal Declaration of Human Rights. Trautmann said that the French had a duty to remember the role of France in the history of slavery in the Americas. The enslavement of Africans in the Americas was a crime against humanity, but resistance to that crime, by the slaves as well as the French Republic, gave birth to a new society on both sides of the Atlantic. She called on the people of France, including those in the Antilles, to celebrate this new society, adding that it was time to recognize the creativity and activism of the Antillean community in metropolitan France itself. That creativity contributed to the greater French community, which would celebrate the abolition under the theme "We were all born in 1848."

Jacques Chirac, the president of France, held one of the first commemorative events at the Elysée Palace in Paris on April 23. Speaking to a large group of French dignitaries, Chirac gave credit for the end of slavery to the French Republic. He said that the revolutionaries of 1789 began a task that was completed by the leaders of the Second Republic in 1848, giving particular credit to Victor Schoelcher, a longtime abolitionist and author of the decrees that ended slavery. Unlike Trautmann, Chirac did not mention actions by the slaves to free themselves, even claiming that Napoleon's troops encountered only "weak resistance" when they reestablished slavery in the colonies in 1802. Instead, Chirac drew attention to what he called the deep commitment of the French Republic to "integration." By freeing the slaves and immediately granting them citizenship, the Republic established a tradition of equality and a French model of integration. The ongoing pursuit of freedom and equality in France today, he said, requires affirmation of the model of integration deployed in 1848.

On April 25, the French Parliament opened an exhibition, entitled *Unchain Your Citizenship* (*Déchaîne ta citoyenneté*), of drawings by thousands of French schoolchildren on the subject of slavery and abolition. The next day Prime Minister Lionel Jospin visited the town of Champagney, in the east of France. In his speech, Jospin said that he had come to Champagney to pay homage to the town's ancestors who, in 1789, asked the king to end slavery in the French colonies. Like Chirac, Jospin called attention to the work of Schoelcher and other abolitionists. Unlike Chirac, Jospin asserted that slavery would not have ended without the revolts of the slaves themselves. He argued that this demonstrated the need for all citizens to actively promote the fundamental values of the Republic. Ensuring freedom for all, he said, required solidarity, equality, and tolerance among people. Jospin added that these values were essential to the French republican model of integration which he, like

Chirac, saw at work in the abolition of slavery. Preserving that model, he said, meant applying those values to immigrants in France.

On April 27, a special ceremony was held at the Pantheon in Paris, where heroes of the French Republic are buried, to honor Victor Schoelcher, the Abbé Grégoire, an abolitionist during the revolution of 1789, and Félix Eboué, the first black French colonial governor, known especially for rallying much of French Africa to the side of the resistance during World War II. Commemorative plaques were unveiled honoring the Haitian revolutionary Toussaint Louverture and the Guadeloupan leader Louis Delgrès, both of whom led resistance to the French restoration of slavery in 1802. Elisabeth Guigou, the minister of justice, delivered a speech calling Louverture and Delgrès heroes of the Republic and added that France could only be true to its ideals if it emphasized openness to all peoples and celebrated cultural diversity.

In Martinique, Guadeloupe, French Guiana, and Réunion, local governments organized dozens of events to commemorate the end of slavery. Although April 27—the anniversary of the passage of the laws ending slavery—was the focal point for events in France, the date varied in the overseas departments. In Martinique, for instance, the end of slavery was marked on May 22, in memory of the slave uprising that effectively ended slavery there before the French decree had been officially announced. Celebrating Martinicans wore shirts emblazoned with the Creole slogan *Nég pété chenn* (Blacks broke their chains).[1] For the first time since the abolition of slavery, a government minister, Jean-Jacques Queyranne, secretary of state for overseas departments and territories, was on hand for the events.[2] In public speeches, Queyranne insisted on the duty to remember slavery and to recognize that French identity had been built out of a mixture of cultures, including those represented in Martinique, which was "inseparable from a desire for equality."[3]

In the Antilles and in France, Antillean activists and intellectuals expressed skepticism regarding the government's efforts to commemorate the abolition of slavery. Some were concerned that the government would primarily celebrate the role French leaders took in liberating the slaves, ignoring the actions the slaves took to liberate themselves.[4] The fact that the bicentennial of the first abolition had not been commemorated in 1994 was cited as giving legitimacy to these concerns.[5] How could Antilleans celebrate the liberation of their ancestors by a government descended from the people who had enslaved them? How could they celebrate, when the government had never acknowledged the role of France in perpetuating slavery and had never made that role explicit in history textbooks?[6] The government is "whitewashing history," one Antillean sociologist remarked.[7]

In Paris on May 23, Antillean skepticism about the French commemoration of the abolition was translated into a large street demonstration. Organized by an alliance of more than three hundred associations, the march was, an organizer remarked, an opportunity for the descendants of slaves to honor their dead while demanding recognition for their community in France.[8] Organizers estimated that twenty thousand people participated in the demonstration, marching silently from the Place de la République to the Place de la Nation in Paris.[9] They carried banners that called into question the official commemorative slogans; instead of "We were all born in 1848," the marchers displayed "We are the sons and daughters of slaves." Other slogans called attention to the economic underdevelopment of the overseas departments and their lack of political autonomy as signs that the abolition of slavery had not really brought about freedom and equality. They demanded that the government recognize that the enslavement of Africans was a crime against humanity. That, one organizer asserted, is an essential step in the fight against racism.[10]

RACE, POLITICS, AND ASSIMILATION

In the context of growing tension concerning racism and immigration in France, the celebration of the abolition of slavery was, for the French government, an opportunity to assert its commitment to freedom and equality for all its citizens. But the real history of that abolition, as Antillean activists were quick to point out, suggested that the commitment was at best ambiguous. Antilleans had long been promised equality in the French Republic, but it never materialized. Although French political leaders argued that there was a "duty to remember" the abolition of slavery, for many Antilleans, the sesquicentennial evoked a much longer memory. They looked back not just on the history of slavery and colonialism, but also on the history of broken French promises of equality and integration. That view of history reflected a far more complex relationship between the Antilles and France than that evoked by the government-sponsored celebration of abolition.

Martinique and Guadeloupe, the last elements of the French colonial empire in the Caribbean, are located in the Lesser Antilles (Figs. 1.1–1.2). Martinique, situated between the independent countries of Dominica and St. Lucia, has been French since 1626. Guadeloupe is just north of Dominica. There are two main islands (Grande Terre and Basse Terre) in what is often humorously referred to as the "Guadeloupan continent," as well as several dependencies, the islands of Marie Galante, Les Saintes, La Désirade, and, as part of its status as a French department, St. Barthelemy and St. Martin (half of which is Dutch) to the north of Antigua. Guadeloupe has been French since 1635.

For most of their history, Martinique and Guadeloupe had much in common with other colonies in the Caribbean. They were characterized by plantation-based economies geared toward the production of sugar and sugar products (e.g., rum) for export to France (see Fig. 3.1). Until the twentieth century, most economic relations were with France and not other islands or

Figure 3.1   Plantation, Martinique.

countries in the Americas, following a French policy known as the *exclusif*, which required that all trade be exclusively with France (Miles 1986, 16). Consequently the French Antilles were economically, politically, and culturally oriented toward France and Europe, not the Caribbean.

As elsewhere in the Americas, the plantation economy was characterized by a small minority of European settlers owning most of the land and by imported African slave labor. In Martinique and Guadeloupe there was a relatively large class of free people of color (*gens de couleur libre*) competing with poorer whites (*petits blancs*), as opposed to the large landholders, (*grands blancs*) for work as overseers, artisans, shopkeepers, and government administrators (Miles 1986, 34; cf. Blérald 1988). Although most people of African descent were slaves on the plantations, some escaped and formed agricultural and fishing villages. French Antillean nationalist ideologies draw heavily on the experiences of these *marrons*.

Antillean society has long been characterized by close linkages between ethnic/racial categories and economic class (Giraud 1979, 10). Although these categories began to blur somewhat in the latter half of the twentieth century, historically, to be black was to be a worker, while whites constituted the propertied classes. The division between black and white has dominated the system of social stratification, but these two groups form the poles of a continuum in which lighter skin color has been associated with greater social prestige. Thus a class of "mixed race" people is situated between the descendants of African

Figure 3.2   Fort-de-France, Martinique. Carnival crowd.

Figure 3.3   Fort-de-France, Martinique. Carnival parade.

slaves (*noirs* or *nègres*) and local whites (known as *békés*). Following the end of slavery in 1848, plantation owners imported indentured workers from Africa (who became known as *nèg congo*) and India (*coulis*) to replace the slaves. In addition, a group known as Syro-Libanais arrived early in the twentieth century to work as shopkeepers and merchants. Finally, throughout their history a certain number of metropolitan French people have been present in the Antilles, most often working as administrators. They are known by various terms (such as *z'oreilles* or *metros*) and are distinguished generally from local whites.

Although the 1789 revolution did not permanently end slavery, the ideologies exported from the *métropole* during the revolution left their mark in the Antilles. Over the course of the nineteenth century, the idea of the Republic became associated, in the view of many Antilleans, with the end of domination by the planters and the end of slavery. The expectation that France and republican ideals held the key to liberation was reinforced with the end of slavery in 1848. For Antilleans of color, the distinction between local whites, who sought to perpetuate their domination, and representatives of the French Republic, who provided the tools for their liberation, was sharpened over the course of the century (Suvélor 1983, 2184, 2187). Anticolonialism became equated with a demand for equal rights in a French Republic. Independence, or local autonomy, represented the continuation of domination by local planters and exclusion of Antilleans of color from participation in government.

At the end of the nineteenth century, the French government established a national school system that could be used to spread republican ideology and create French citizens out of the diverse people in France. The same national school system was established at the same time in the French Antilles. It contributed to the growth of both republican ideology and the spread of the idea that assimilation into French society would lead to greater freedom and power for people of color (Constant 1988, 44). Just as the Catholic right resisted the creation of secular schools in France, the *békés* fought against them in the Antilles, seeing them as a threat to their domination. Education became, in the Antilles, an important part of the political agenda of those who sought greater assimilation of the Antilles into France (Blérald 1988, 92).

But the establishment of the Republic's secular schools meant that local history, culture, and language were absent from the curriculum. Young Antilleans learned of "their ancestors the Gauls," rather than the history of Martinique and Guadeloupe, and in some cases local subjects were actively suppressed. Thus the use of Creole, the first language of most Guadeloupans and Martinicans, was forbidden in the schools, just as the use of local languages was forbidden in metropolitan provincial schools.[11] Successful education in the schools of the Republic meant identification with Parisian cultural models and acceptance of the notion that to have a legitimate political voice, one had to accept the ideology of the Republic (Blérald 1988, 92).

Figure 3.4   Martinique.

Figure 3.5   Martinique.

Politics in the Antilles underwent significant transformations in the last decades of the nineteenth century, with the establishment of the Third Republic in France. Beginning in the 1870s, the Antilles were once more represented in the French National Assembly. Local assemblies were dominated by members of the colored bourgeoisie rather than white planters. Universal suffrage and legislative identity with France—the same laws applied in the same manner—became the key demands of the bourgeoisie of color. Depending on the French Republic for their legitimacy, the politicians of color in the Antilles were more interested in greater assimilation into France than in independence. Efforts to gain departmental status for Martinique and Guadeloupe became the principal political goal of Antillean political leaders in the decades prior to World War II (Constant 1988).

The Third Republic provided a context and mechanisms by which the French Antilles were progressively brought into the same cultural and administrative framework as metropolitan France. Theoretically at least, Antilleans began to think of themselves as citizens of the Republic like those in metropolitan France. This movement toward complete assimilation reached its high point after World War II with the "departmentalization" of Martinique and Guadeloupe (along with French Guiana and Réunion). In the context of postwar France, the demands of Antillean representatives in the National Assembly led to the passage of a law in 1946, transforming Martinique and Guadeloupe into *départements d'outre-mer* (overseas departments) and presumably completing the legal assimilation of the Antilles.

Guadeloupe and Martinique are, thus, integrated more or less completely in French political and administrative systems. Theoretically, the overseas departments are simply extensions of the *métropole,* represented like any other department in the National Assembly, with the same legal system, the same administrative statutes, and no trade barriers. Instead of a colonial governor, the Paris government is represented on each island by a prefect, with authority similar to those in the departments of the *métropole.* Since departmentalization, French government ministries have also established local offices, rather than working through the colonial administration. The locally elected Conseil Général, a legislative body at the departmental level, has the same powers as do those in metropolitan France. The Conseil Régional, another locally elected body, is also constituted like its metropolitan counterparts except that it deals with exactly the same territory as the Conseil Général, unlike similar bodies in the *métropole.* Finally, social legislation, such as family allocations for children, unemployment payments, and health care, are applied in the Antilles just as in France, although until the 1990s, Antilleans received lower levels of payments than metropolitan beneficiaries (see Constant and Daniel 1997).

Despite official legal assimilation, there have long been some legal differences between France and the Antilles. Social welfare payments were, until recently, lower in the Antilles than in France, as was the minimum wage. However, civil servants were paid a 40 percent supplement to their salaries for working in the Antilles. The ministry that dealt with the colonies has been replaced with a ministry for overseas departments and territories, so that there was—and still is—a separate administration for the overseas departments, whose role is to coordinate the activities of all the other administrations there. Local government in the Antilles has long been financed through mechanisms that are distinct from those in the *métropole* (Daniel 1997; Nosel 1997; François-Lubin 1997).

In demanding departmentalization, Antillean political leaders of the 1930s and 1940s sought to guarantee equal political rights for people of color under the orderly rule of French law. In this area at least, departmentalization has largely succeeded. They also hoped that by bringing the Antilles into the same legal framework as the *métropole,* they could break the economic power of the *békés* and, with government aid, raise living standards for Antilleans to European levels. Here the success of departmentalization is less evident. Although the standard of living is high relative to the rest of the Caribbean, Antillean incomes and wealth are still below the levels of metropolitan France. The *békés* continue to wield considerable economic power (Nosel 1997).

The economic structures of Martinique and Guadeloupe have been profoundly transformed since departmentalization, but these changes are not necessarily viewed by Antilleans as fulfilling the promise of assimilation. The most significant change has been the nearly total destruction of the plantation economy: the French Antilles are today heavily service-based economies. In the early 1960s, close to 40 percent of the working-age population was employed in agriculture; by the beginning of the 1980s it was less than 10 percent. The trend in the tertiary sector has closely reflected that of the primary sector. Around 10 percent of the active population worked in services in the early 1960s. In the 1980s, that figure had risen to just over 30 percent.

Departmentalization is to a large extent responsible for these changes. First, by bringing the Antilles in line with French social legislation, labor costs have risen dramatically since the 1940s. Coupled with growing competition for European markets by tropical products from African and Latin American countries, most of the Antillean plantations could no longer compete. At the same time, departmentalization has brought with it the implantation of large French bureaucracies to administer social services. By 1980, nearly 30 percent of the working population of Martinique held jobs in government services, and city hall in Fort-de-France was reputed to be the island's biggest employer, surpassing the sugar producers in total employees.[12]

The standard of living of Martinique and Guadeloupe has risen dramatically as well. These are consumer societies, like the *métropole,* with well-stocked French supermarket chains, furniture stores, and automobile dealerships. The Antilles are deeply dependent on France for the importation of consumer goods, since local production is inadequate (Miles 1995). A large part of the incomes that are devoted to the purchase of these goods result from government spending, whether highly salaried functionaries or continual heavy government investment in infrastructure (Giraud and Jamard 1982; Miles 1995; Nosel 1997; François-Lubin 1997).

The French Antilles suffer from high unemployment rates, an estimated 25–30 percent of the population is without regular work (Conconne 2003).[13] Yet people have high expectations concerning employment and standards of living, just as in metropolitan France. Few Antilleans are interested in working in the agricultural sector, which pays low wages and has recruited large immigrant populations from other parts of the Caribbean (Brodwin 2003a). Meanwhile, since the early 1960s, both Guadeloupe and Martinique have experienced considerable out-migration to metropolitan France.

The demand for greater assimilation into France began with the hope that Antilleans could be liberated from political and economic domination by the békés. But many have come to regard departmentalization as a kind of Faustian bargain. In exchange for partial liberation from the power of local whites, the local economy has been destroyed, leaving a largely French-controlled consumer economy instead. French assimilation policy has also been criticized for eliminating much that was culturally distinct about the Antilles. In an era when most former colonies—including most of the Caribbean—have become independent, the departmental status of Martinique and Guadeloupe seems at least incongruous and at worst a form of neocolonialism. Finally, without a growing local economy, thousands of Antilleans have migrated since the 1960s to metropolitan France, constituting what is often referred to as a "third island" there. All of this combines to make many Antilleans suspicious of French policymakers, especially when they wish to celebrate the abolition of slavery with slogans such as "We were all born in 1848."

THE VIEW FROM FRANCE

Antilleans are not the only people skeptical of their effective assimilation into France. Among metropolitan French people, there is a somewhat ambiguous attitude toward the status of the Antilles as French departments. When I tell French friends of my interest in people from France's "colonies," most are quick to point out that the Antilles are departments, not colonies. But the Antilles are rarely considered part of France when metropolitan French people examine their own history, economy, or geography. While French policies have operated to encourage Antillean aspirations to assimilate into the French nation, metropolitan ideas of the exotic tropics, and the people who live in them, have worked to maintain a sense of difference.

Difficulties in deciding exactly how to think about Antilleans have been evident in France for some time. The problem posed by the identity of the

inhabitants of the French Antilles was examined soon after departmentalization in the early 1950s by the French anthropologist Michel Leiris. Leiris's
project was to examine a situation of what he called "culture contact" in order to discover how these islands could be successfully assimilated as French
departments (Leiris 1955). In the introduction to his study, Leiris argued
that if Antilleans were to be fully integrated into France, they needed both legal equality and policies that would integrate them into the cultural life of
the nation. But Leiris suggested that the problem of assimilation only applied
to groups of "non-European" origin; the other inhabitants of the islands—
primarily the white planters—remained culturally French over the centuries.
Nonetheless, Leiris found it difficult to determine whether or not the Antilles
were French, African, or something new.

The idea that Martinicans and Guadeloupans have a problematic cultural
identity has not changed since Leiris did his study. As the remnants of a colonial empire that has separated into many independent states, the French Antilles are anomalies in the eyes of many metropolitan French people. Because
the Antilles remain part of France in a postcolonial era, French analysts often
conclude that there is something wrong with them. French social scientists
who have studied the Antilles frequently propose that the history of colonialism and ongoing dependence on France has made a "normal" cultural life
and social structure impossible in the islands. As long as the Antilles remain
tied to France, these analysts argue, they will not develop "healthy" cultures.
Instead, they will remain characterized by what French analysts believe they
lack: "normal" kinship structures, political autonomy, individualism; all qualities that are essential to French national identity (André 1983; Affergan 1983;
cf. Burton 1994).

If the Antilles are problematic for metropolitan French intellectuals, they
also represent more general ideas of the exotic. Even while denouncing the
oppressive French authorities that ruled Martinique during World War II,
both anthropologist Claude Lévi-Strauss (1973) and the surrealist writer André Breton (1972) described Martinique mostly in terms of splendid jungles
and surreal volcanoes. In a collection of essays about Martinique and Guadeloupe in the journal *Autrement*, a journalist noted that the people of these
tropical islands live in a natural setting that is "sweet and exuberant, sometimes violent" and that they are capable of producing a "secret alchemy"
through the "omnipresent vitality" of the setting. They speak a language full
of life and images that, as it moves from island to island, "vibrates to the
rhythms, sounds, scents and colors that form their interior music" (Bastien
1989, 11). This exotic view is applied even to efforts by Antilleans to represent
their own cultural distinctiveness. When three Martinican intellectuals
(Bernabé et al. 1989) published a manifesto for a new literary and political
movement in the late 1980s, it was reviewed in the French press with food

metaphors—the manifesto was described as a recipe for a ray in ginger sauce—rather than as a serious effort at political self-definition.[14]

For most metropolitan French people, the Antilles represent stereotypes of the tropics, places of magic, mystery, and sexual vitality. Antilleans in France are not seen as ordinary French citizens but as representatives of a foreign culture, dependent on France but different from it. At best they are the carriers of entertaining dance music, at worst they are noisy neighbors—the stereotypes commonly used to describe other immigrant groups. Social scientists who specialize in the French Antilles are understood, in France, to be specialists in the Caribbean, not France. In popular representations, Antillean cultures are reduced to exotic color, which is something less than the high culture represented by French artistic performances and very different from representations of the regional folk cultures of France.

The idea that the Antilles are not really French probably explained why the French historian dismissed my assertion that the abolition of slavery in the Antilles in 1848 was important for France. The subsequent commemoration of that abolition in 1998 did not originate in a sudden desire by the French government to fulfill the promise of assimilation. Instead, the 1998 celebration reflected the government's desire to make a promise of integration to immigrants in contemporary France and to demonstrate that France's fundamental values were those of freedom and equality, not racism and xenophobia. Despite more than fifty years of assimilation policies, the Antilles are still not considered to be French in the same way as the departments of metropolitan France. Antilleans, when they move to France, are well aware of these distinctions.

CROSSING THE ATLANTIC

Numbering approximately 337,000, Martinicans and Guadeloupans form one of the larger immigrant groups in metropolitan France (Marie 2002, 32; Boëldieu and Borrel 2000, 2). But the number of Antilleans in France is especially significant when compared with the populations of Martinique and Guadeloupe. According to the 1999 census, Martinique's population was 381,427, while there were 422,496 people in Guadeloupe. Close to a third of the people who can consider themselves Antillean live in France. This means that policy issues, from economic development to cultural assimilation, have significance not only in the Caribbean but in metropolitan France as well. In 1983, for instance, the government made the date of the abolition of slavery a holiday in the overseas departments but not in France. With sizable populations from those departments living in France, many Antillean activists question why no such holiday has been decreed there as well. Just as departmentalization has led to an ambiguous assimilation into France, migration has made many Antilleans less certain of their place in French society.

The Antillean population in the *métropole* presents characteristics that distinguish it from other labor migrations, as well as from the general metropolitan French population. Most labor migrations start out with a majority of men, followed by women joining their husbands rather than initially seeking employment. This has not been the case with Antilleans. A slight majority of Antillean migrants since the early 1960s have been women; more Antillean women in France work than either French women or women in the Antilles (Marie 2002, 28). Antillean migrants are heavily employed in the service sector—more than half work in the French administration, local government, or other public services. While they are concentrated in relatively unskilled low-wage jobs—nurse's aides, police, customs agents, museum guards, mail sorters, and subway workers—they have job security and benefits not generally available to other immigrants.

Over 70 percent of Antilleans living in France live in the Paris region (Marie 1993a, 12). Public sector employment has allowed many of them to gain access to moderately priced public housing, which traditionally was considered to be superior to much of the private rental housing available in the region. In recent decades, however, these large housing complexes have come to be seen as the source of social tension in large French cities, associated with crime, immigration, and poverty. A majority of Antilleans in France still live in these complexes, which are the subject of many of the most fraught policy debates in contemporary France (Marie 1993b, 10).

The children of Antillean immigrants in France have not had the same experiences as their parents. With the growth of unemployment in France since the 1970s, it has become much more difficult to get access to the kind of public sector jobs their parents have, even if they are French citizens. In addition, they are often victims of the same kind of racial discrimination in housing and employment experienced by other immigrants. Yet as French citizens, the children of Antillean immigrants—often referred to as the second generation—are mostly invisible to policymakers. They are not included in the policy debates on immigration, nor are they taken into consideration when policy toward the Antilles is considered.

The perception of Antilleans as not quite foreign and not quite French has been heightened by French policies on Antillean migration since the early 1960s. There have long been Antilleans in France; prior to the 1960s, the population was small, consisting mostly of university students, intellectuals, and government administrators. After 1962, the government began to actively recruit Antilleans to work in France. At that time, the Bureau pour le développement des migrations intéressant les départements d'outre-mer (Bureau for the Development of Migrations from the Overseas Departments, BUMIDOM) was created to recruit Antillean migrants to France. In the late 1950s, the Antilles experienced rapid population growth and labor unrest, as the economy experienced shifts following departmentalization. In France there were labor

Figure 3.6   Paris suburbs.

shortages in the public sector. The BUMIDOM was created to address both of these problems, importing thousands of Antilleans for work in France.

By the early 1980s, the BUMIDOM had developed a reputation for a narrow focus on bringing Antilleans to France without preparing them for their new life and without contributing to economic development in the Antilles. Its policies seemed increasingly out of touch with the experiences of Antilleans in France and with the demands of Antilleans in the Antilles. The growth of unemployment in France in the 1970s, along with greater attention to the cultural distinctiveness of immigrants, led to the creation of a new agency, the Agence nationale pour l'insertion et la promotion des travailleurs d'outre-mer (National Agency for the Promotion and Insertion of Workers from Overseas, ANT), which replaced the BUMIDOM in 1982. The ANT was still charged with assisting Antilleans with migration to France, but its mission was expanded to include assisting return migrants, helping Antilleans start businesses, and encouraging the development of nonprofit organizations among Antilleans in France that could serve as relays for government policies (Constant 1997, 116).

Nonprofit associations in France are regulated by a 1901 law on freedom of association and consequently are called "1901 law associations." An organization in France that is publicly designated as a 1901 law association is a serious group with official recognition. Until the early 1980s, noncitizens could join but could not lead such associations. When that was changed in 1981, there was a veritable explosion in the number of associations organized and led by immigrants in France. As citizens, Antilleans have always been able to form 1901 law associations and have done so frequently in the Antilles. In France, however, there was little organizing among Antilleans until the early 1980s, when other immigrants also began to organize. Since then, hundreds of Antillean nonprofit organizations have been formed.

There are a number of explanations for this development. The creation of the ANT, with its policy of subsidizing Antillean associations, has certainly played a role. In addition, Antilleans may have been inspired by the growth of nonprofit organizations among other immigrant groups. The realization that they had become permanent residents of France and were unlikely to return to the islands may have encouraged many Antillean immigrants to begin to organize in France. But the growing number of Antillean organizations in France also results from the experience of racism in France, whether job and housing discrimination, police harassment, or hostility from French people.

Even as they organize, however, many Antilleans recognize that gaining cultural recognition from the French government is fraught with ambiguity. The idea of recognition runs against the grain of a deep-seated ideology of assimilation that older Antilleans especially have long understood as the pre-ferred path toward equality in France. Yet most Antilleans recognize that the assimilation of the Antilles has never been successful. The continued relative underdevelopment of the islands and the existence of separate government agencies to deal with them is a tacit recognition of their distinctiveness. Antil-leans settled in France, no longer exactly Antillean in the eyes of the govern-ment but not quite French either, risk becoming invisible without gaining the benefits of real assimilation.

WHAT IS AN ANTILLEAN?

The historical depth and institutional ties between Martinique, Guadeloupe, and France make it difficult to conceive of them as culturally distinct from one another. Martinican novelist and social critic Edouard Glissant has sug-gested that the French Antilles have no "cultural hinterland" (*arrière-pays cul-turel*), no precolonial cultural space to call their own (1981, 166). Confronted with the contradictions of their incorporation in France, Antillean activists and intellectuals have created a number of alternative ways of thinking about what it means to be Antillean. These ideologies have developed in close rela-tion with some of the dominant ways of thinking about identity in France, but they have also been influenced by anticolonial movements around the world. They provide some of the basic ideas used by Antillean activists in contemporary France.

One of the first movements to challenge French ideas about Antilleans, as well as about other black people, started in the 1920s and 1930s among Antillean and African students in Paris. Called *negritude*, the movement published two short-lived journals, *Légitime défense* and *L'Etudiant noir*, where many of their ideas were first publicized. Led by Léon Gontron Damas (from French Guiana), Léopold Senghor (from Senegal), and Aimé Césaire (from Martinique), the promoters of *négritude* sought to denounce colonialism as a movement that dehumanized and devalued subjugated peoples. To counter this, they chose to assert a black identity. The basic ideology of *négritude* started with the observation that the subordination of black peoples occurred through the imposition of European *culture* on colonized peoples. The means to liberation was through affirmation of black *culture*, the assertion of "blackness" in the arts and in politics (Blérald 1981, 37). The ideology of *négritude* became the framework for some of the best known and most widely read Francophone literature. Césaire's *cahier d'un retour au pays natal* (*Notebook of a return to the native land*), for example, provided inspiration for the anticolonial movement in the decades that followed (1983, 2001).

In an apparent paradox, one of the leaders of this movement, Aimé Césaire, become an important proponent of departmentalization in the 1940s. He argued that *négritude* was not so much a movement that rejected all Western values in favor of African values as it was a denunciation of a process of assimilation that would leave one group subordinate to another (Blérald 1981, 74). For Césaire and his colleagues, the objective of their movement was to make African values equal to European values, so that cultural divisions would no longer provide fuel for racism. In short, *négritude* became a humanist rather than a nationalist ideology (Césaire 1983, 50). By making his African and European heritages equal, Césaire could be comfortable drawing on France's revolutionary promise of equality when demanding departmentalization.

As a basis of Antillean identity, *négritude* has been subject to many attacks since departmentalization. One significant attack has come from those who have proposed another way of thinking about Antillean identity, *antillanité*, which can be translated as "Caribbean-ness." For Edouard Glissant (1981, 35), a Martinican intellectual, *négritude* was positive because it reminded Antilleans of their African heritage. He argues, however, that this is only a first step, a detour from which Antilleans must return in order to develop their own identity in a specifically Antillean context. In his view, the Martinican anticolonial activist Frantz Fanon represented the most extreme case of this detour, since Fanon actually committed his life to the cause of decolonization in Africa, working for the unity of all colonized people. Although Fanon used many Antillean examples in his analysis of the alienation caused by colonialism, the fact that he never sought to "return" to work in Martinique made it impossible, according to Glissant, for his work to contribute significantly to the creation of Antillean identity (Glissant 1981, 36; cf. Fanon 1952).

Despite his criticism of Fanon, Glissant bases his analysis of Antillean societies on a similar notion of the alienation caused by colonialism. The French

Antilles, argues Glissant (1981, 167), are culturally "morbid" because they are entirely dependent on outsiders—the French—for the goods they consume, both in material and symbolic terms. The history of slavery and assimilation has left the Antilles without a sense of their own cultural identity, separate from that of their colonizers. Without such an identity, they risk disappearing entirely within the dominant French *culture*, a process he calls "cultural genocide." To redress this situation, he argues (1981, 178) that it is necessary to restructure Martinican and Guadeloupan economies within the context of a greater Caribbean economy. In addition, artistic production must become grounded in a creative search for identity in popular *culture*. Rather than reduce popular *culture* to "folklore," which keeps an Antillean identity subordinate to French *culture*, Glissant (1981, 183) argues for the grounding of art in the reality of popular *culture*, thus making artistic production the production of a national identity.

Both *négritude* and *antillanité* are theories that focus primarily on the formation of counterdiscourses to the French ideology of assimilation. Thus Césaire tied his political project to artistic production, seen as a means of getting beyond the "obvious order of things" to develop a more insightful perspective on the formation of Antillean identity (Blérald 1981, 71). Similarly, Glissant seemed determined to form an Antillean discursive space separate from that of the French. Both of these movements seek to link their artistic proposals to an analysis of the material reality of life in the Antilles, usually through a Marxist or nationalist perspective. In contrast, more recent attempts to develop an understanding of Antillean identity have focused almost entirely on issues related to cultural identity, leaving any nationalist or materialist ideologies to the side.

The most significant example of this can be found in a manifesto written by three Martinican intellectuals, Jean Bernabé, Patrick Chamoiseau, and Raphaël Confiant, in which they elaborate a concept called *créolité* (Bernabé et al. 1989). While most Antillean activists are familiar with *négritude* and *antillanité*, neither ideology seemed particularly exciting or innovative by the late 1980s. *Créolité*, however, speaks to the experiences of Antilleans in France. The manifesto, *Eloge de la Créolité* (*In Praise of Creoleness*), first published in 1989, was presented in public during the Festival Caraibe in the Parisian suburb of St. Denis in May 1988. The concepts it presented quickly gained attention in both France and the French Antilles. At a conference in Paris the following December, I heard Pierre Pinalie, a French linguist who lives and teaches in Martinique, argue that the formation of Caribbean identities based on either African descent—*négritude*—or on the specificity of the Caribbean—*antillanité*—should be replaced by the idea of *créolité*. This idea, he claimed, pointed to the cultural creativity of Caribbean diaspora communities in France, as well as the United States and the United Kingdom. By escaping the racial and geographic boundaries imposed by earlier ideas about

Caribbean identities, *créolité* would make better sense of the experiences of Antilleans in both the Caribbean and France.

Raphael Confiant and Patrick Chamoiseau spoke at a public fundraiser for an Antillean radio station in January 1989. The radio station, managed by a nonprofit Antillean association, had recently lost its license to a rival group. Although both groups were Antillean, their political and economic orientations were different. The organizers of the fundraiser wanted a radio station that promoted the idea of an "authentic" Antillean community in Paris, drawing on nonprofit associations to produce a wide range of programs, including news, religious affairs, political and social commentary, as well as music. The group that had just won the license, they claimed, was primarily interested in musical programming that would sell advertising.

Held at the Institute for Latin American Studies in a rather upscale part of central Paris, the event attracted over one hundred people, many belonging to prominent Antillean associations in Paris. Confiant and Chamoiseau, the evening's featured speakers, had attracted a great deal of critical acclaim in France in the late 1980s with novels that drew on the techniques of magical realism and a creative mixture of Creole and French in ways that seemed destined to revive a sterile French literary scene (see Chamoiseau 1986, 1992; Confiant 1988). Confiant opened the conference with a greeting in Creole, then shifted into French, asserting that many of the people in the overwhelmingly Antillean audience probably did not understand Creole. The problem with using French, he asserted, is that it cannot accurately represent the Antillean reality. We Antilleans, he added, are all bilingual but one of our languages is "maternal" and the other is "adopted." If we wish to remain "authentic," then we must exercise great care when using French. As authors, he said, he and Chamoiseau are both caught between the need to write in French if they wish to be read, and the need to express a reality that is fundamentally Creole.

The French language has been the historic vehicle of a cultural message that systematically denied the importance of Creole language and culture, Chamoiseau added. The story of Antillean writing and identity movements, he said, is one of constant struggle against that domination. Thus Césaire, with Senghor and Damas, developed the idea of *négritude* as a means to reassert the value of black cultures in the face of colonialism. Reasserting the value of black cultures and Africa was, in Confiant and Chamoiseau's view, a necessary step, but also a problematic one, because it also created what they called the "Africanist illusion." *Négritude* replaced the cultural focus on France with a similar focus on Africa, simply shifting the focus of Antilleans from one ancestor to another. Edouard Glissant provided the next necessary step, from Africa back to the Caribbean. Glissant's concept of *antillanité* provided, in their view, a real rupture with other forms of identity, calling on Antilleans to focus on their place in the Caribbean.

However, Confiant and Chamoiseau felt that Glissant's project was too anchored in the Caribbean and too close to a nationalism that is a reflection of European ideas. Having accepted Glissant's suggestion that Antillean artists need to explore their cultural specificity, they declared that Antilleans are the product of a constant interaction of ideas and peoples from all over the world, not some sort of hermetically sealed local culture. In the *Eloge* they wrote, "We are everything at once. We are Europe and Africa, but we have been raised on the contributions of Asia and the Levant and of India. We carry survivals of pre-Columbian America as well. *Créolité* is 'the world, diffracted and recomposed'" (Bernabé et al. 1989, 27). They argued against the "false universalism" proposed by the French and by third world nationalists, suggesting that cultural diversity must be preserved through an open exchange between cultures (Bernabé et al. 1989, 28). They defined three objectives for their project. First, Antilleans must continue to explore their own oral tradition in order to preserve the cultural specificity they have created. Second, they should work through the rewriting of history to produce a history of the development of their own culture. Finally, having affirmed their own culture, they will be prepared to contribute to a global understanding of the human condition.

For Antilleans in Paris, *créolité*, with its emphasis on the creation of something new out of European and African roots, seemed inspiring and legitimizing. It provided them with ideological tools to make sense of their distinctiveness within French society. They were not like other immigrant groups, defined by a culture of origin easily distinguished from that of France, but they were not simply French either. Rather than struggle to create a new kind of national identity, *créolité* promoted the idea that Antillean identities were a new and cutting-edge form of identity, something that went beyond French and immigrant identities. Ways of thinking about identity proposed by French leaders were obsolete in this view.

BETRAYED ANTILLES

The 1998 commemoration of the abolition of slavery could have been an occasion for the French government to acknowledge the history of broken promises to the Antilles. But Antilleans were understandably suspicious of the actions of the government. They suspected that the commemoration had less to do with the history of slavery than with the concerns about French republican values in the context of debates about immigration. Although Antilleans have long been part of France, they are still not French. Even when they sought assimilation into the Republic, expressing a willingness to put aside their own cultural particularities in order to gain access to the freedom and equality that are fundamental republican values, the French response was at best ambiguous. In the 1998 commemoration, French people were exhorted to "unchain their citizenship." But Antilleans know that membership in the French Republic is limited, that their citizenship is still "in chains."

The Antillean demand for assimilation was rooted in nineteenth-century efforts to free Antilleans of color from the domination of local white plantation owners. But in the years after World War II, anticolonial movements did not demand greater equality within empires. They demanded independence. The failure of Antilleans to seek independence made them strange in the view of many French analysts, perhaps pathological. This view, along with an understanding of the Antilles as sensual, exotic playgrounds, has meant that Antilleans are rarely viewed as French. Yet by virtue of their citizenship, Antilleans in France have become largely invisible in the debates over immigration since the 1980s. Their long-term loyalty to France has earned them neither equality nor cultural recognition.

Since the 1930s, Antillean intellectuals have worked to make sense of their place in the Caribbean and in France. Ideologies such as *négritude* and *antillanité* have provided alternatives to the dominant ideology of assimilation. While those ideas may have inspired political activists in the Antilles, they did not, in the late 1980s, address the situation of Antilleans living in France. In the 1980s and 1990s, *créolité* provided an appealing new approach to identity for Antilleans in France. By demanding recognition for the originality of Antillean artistic culture and history, *créolité* works to erase the idea that Antillean societies are not "normal." At the same time, by asserting that the Antilles represent the future of all societies, *créolité* allows Antilleans in France to see themselves as more than "just" another immigrant group. They are representatives of a cultural avant-garde. They have moved beyond Frenchness.

Notes

1. Marie-France Rouze, *Agence France Presse*, May 22, 1998.

2. In France a secretary of state is a junior member of the cabinet.

3. Rouze, *Agence France Presse*, May 22, 1998. See Bongie 2001; Chivallon 2002; Miles 1999; Price 2001; and Schmidt 1999 for analyses of commemorations in Martinique and Guadeloupe.

4. Daniel Maximin, interview, *Le Monde*, April 24, 1998.

5. Philippe-Jean Catinchi, *Le Monde*, April 24, 1998.

6. Annick Cojean, *Le Monde*, April 27, 1998.

7. Claude-Valentin Marie, quoted by Béatrice Bantman in *Libération*, April 25, 1998; cf. Ina Césaire, "A chacun sa commémoration," *Libération*, April 25, 1998.

8. Serge Romana, quoted in *Alizés*, June–September 1998.

9. *Le Monde*, May 26, 1998. The police estimated the crowd at 8,000.

10. Serge Romana, quoted in *Alizés*, June–September 1998. In 1999, the National Assembly passed a law making slavery a crime against humanity.

11. Joseph Zobel (1974) and Raphaël Confiant (1988) have written novels that provide excellent descriptions of the role of the schools in creating Frenchmen out of Martinicans. See Fanon (1952, 13–32) for an interesting examination of the symbolism of language use in the context of assimilationist ideas in the Antilles. It is interesting to compare these Antillean representations of cultural alienation with a metropolitan provincial example, Hélias 1978.

12. The figures in this paragraph come from Miles 1986 (on Martinique alone); Bastien 1989b; Crusol 1975; and Giraud and Jamard 1982.

13. See also Lamia Oualalou, "Le premier ministre arrive ce soir en Martinique; L'économie antillaise à la dérive," *Le Figaro*, October 27, 1999; Browne 2002.

14. *Libération*, July 24 1989, 17–19.

Further Reading

Bernabé, Jean, Patrick Chamoiseau, and Raphaël Confiant. 1993. *Eloge de la Créolité: In Praise of Creoleness*. Translated by M. B. Taleb-Khyar. Paris: Gallimard. The manifesto that started the *créolité* movement.

Burton, Richard D. E., and Fred Réno, eds. 1995. *French and West Indian: Martinique, Guadeloupe, and French Guiana Today*. Charlottesville: University Press of Virginia. A collection of essays evaluating the state of French Antillean societies as they become more integrated into the European Union.

Césaire, Aimé. 2001. *Notebook of a Return to the Native Land*. Translated and edited by Clayton Eshleman and Annette Smith. Middletown, Conn.: Wesleyan University Press. Written by the most famous intellectual and political leader in Martinique, this poem, a searing critique of colonialism, is one of the founding documents of the negritude movement.

Fanon, Frantz. 1967. *Black Skin, White Masks*. Translated by Charles Lam Markmann. New York: Grove. Written by a Martinican who became an internationally recognized anticolonial activist, this is a classic analysis of the psychological effects of colonialism on people in the Caribbean.

Glissant, Edouard. 1989. *Caribbean Discourse: Selected Essays*. Translated and edited by J. Michael Dash. Charlottesville: University Press of Virginia. A collection of essays that forms the starting point for the idea of *antillanité*.

CHAPTER FOUR

BOUDIN, RHUM, AND *ZOUK*: PERFORMANCE AND CULTURAL CONFRONTATION

STAGING BLOOD AND NOSTALGIA

In March 1989, I attended a performance by the Paris-based Antillean theater troupe Eloge in Colombes, a working-class suburb of Paris. The troupe had been invited to perform by a local Antillean association as part of an evening that was otherwise devoted to a visit from the mayor of Colombes, who was running for re-election. Since most French politicians did little to reach out to potential ethnic voting blocs, the mayor's visit was unusual. It appeared to signal growing attention to the demands of the diverse immigrants in Colombes and neighboring towns. Local activists hoped that the Eloge performance would bring out Antilleans who might not otherwise be interested in local politics and impress the mayor with the community's size and organization. The evening would begin with the play, followed by a discussion with the mayor. By beginning with the performance, organizers hoped to set a distinctly Antillean framework for the evening, drawing the mayor onto their cultural terrain.

Things did not work out as planned. The mayor arrived late and apologized for a busy schedule of campaign stops. He then asked to speak first, pre-empting the play. He spoke of Martinique and Guadeloupe in a patronizing tone. None of the programs he promised to implement were targeted to the Antillean community; indeed, he dismissed demands to address their needs as illegitimate. The mayor also denied the existence of racism in Colombes, arguing that Antilleans could not be victims of racism because they are citizens. He criticized Antilleans for making too much noise in public housing. After a sharp exchange with the audience, the mayor and his entourage left, taking with them much of the goodwill generated by his willingness to meet with Antilleans.[1]

With the mayor gone, Eloge took the stage. The scenery evoked a plantation house on an island like Guadeloupe or Martinique—a dining table, four chairs, a couch, and two additional chairs around a low coffee table with a lamp made from a puffer fish. Several sheets of wallpaper with photographs of French doors opening onto a verdant tropical landscape and two large travel posters of Martinique and Guadeloupe provided backdrops. Costumes reminded the audience of Antillean "traditional" clothing. The actress playing the role of the family servant wore a dress made from the madras cloth one sees in paintings for tourists. The man playing the father and plantation owner dressed in jeans, wore a pith helmet, and carried a machete.

The play, written by an Eloge member, had a rather melodramatic title, *Et le sang gicla* (*And the blood spurts*)—a tragic story of lost love wrapped up in a comedy of manners. A young black Antillean woman falls in love with the son of a wealthy white *béké*. The young woman's family owns a sugar plantation beset with labor disputes and financial problems. The difficulties faced in managing the plantation—stereotypically lazy, belligerent, drunken workers—provide a comic backdrop to the parents' concerns about their daughter's choice of suitor. The parents discuss (in French, while the workers speak Creole) their daughter's marital prospects. Will she marry someone with enough money to help support the plantation?

They invite her suitor to dinner and learn that his intentions toward their daughter seem honorable. He holds a position of some importance in a bank; the parents are overjoyed. The parents propose a round of toasts and the father asks the young man his family name. Unknown to the suitor, his white grandfather had killed the uncle of his bride-to-be, her father's brother—a black man—because he wished to marry his daughter. The mother and daughter argue that such disputes are a thing of the past. But the father swears that his daughter will never marry anyone from that family and storms offstage.

In the next act, the groom, still hopeful, attempts to convince his love to elope, wooing her with tales of Paris, where they can be free of racial conflicts. She is willing, but it is too late. Her father, returning from the fields, sees them together and kills the young man with his machete. He is stunned at his action and immediately remorseful, but there is no time to make amends. The daughter runs offstage and a shot is heard. She is dead.

Even on the institutional stage of a cold municipal auditorium, this melodrama enchanted the audience. The play was filled with small vignettes that echoed the follies of rural life in Guadeloupe and Martinique. Sarcastic Creole asides from the maid concerning minor household manias, parental rejection of suitors, fears about interracial dating, comments from drunken workers, the father's penny-pinching concerns when a worker is injured—all evoked a Caribbean world the audience had left behind.

Riding in the last train back to Paris with members of Eloge, I asked about what the mayor had said and about the audience reaction to the play. The mayor, someone responded, does not understand our lives here or where we come from. He should have seen the play before speaking, another added. "*Le culturel*," she concluded, "is really the best way to express a way of life."

CULTURE: HIGH, FOLK, OR FETISH?

Who could fail to understand them after that? *Le culturel*, as portrayed in performances of the Eloge Theater Troupe, was defined in narrow artistic terms. Theater, dance, music, and art were included as privileged forms with which to represent Antillean life. Yet why turn to the arts as the major means for representation of Antillean lives? Did the idea of *le culturel* refer to the representations or to the people whose lives are represented? Why were those lives situated in Guadeloupe and Martinique more often than in metropolitan France? Why not represent lives like those of people in the theater troupe, who lived mostly in the Paris region and not across the Atlantic? If the performers believed that greater understanding would come through exposure to *le culturel*, why did Eloge perform primarily in front of Antillean audiences? Who were they trying to convince—and of what—by presenting their plays? What is the relationship between Antillean *culture* and French national *culture*?

Plays, literature, and other performing arts are central to the representation of Antillean identities in Martinique and Guadeloupe. The main object of political action in the Antilles in recent decades has been to turn Martinicans and Guadeloupans into "cultural citizens," people deeply aware of each island's history and traditions (Murray 2002; cf. Giraud 1999). The French government has also worked to promote French cultural citizenship. Artistic production has historically played an important role in the formation of ideas about what constitutes the French nation and having a national cultural policy—policies that subsidize and organize the arts—is as much a part of French government as having a military. The Ministry of Culture has been a cabinet-level position since 1959, and it has spent millions of francs annually on the development, promotion, and defense of French arts. The French state organizes and funds arts organizations, including theaters, museums, movie studios, and a wide range of other groups. That France should have a national impact on the world in artistic as well as political and economic terms is considered a significant aspect of what makes France a great nation. In the 1980s, the Ministry of Culture directed the construction of the series of "grand projects," including the Bastille Opera, the new national library, and the expansion of the Louvre, among many others, that were showcased with the celebration of the bicentennial of the French Revolution. The Ministry of Culture is also charged with defending French *culture* against the invasion of globalized, especially American, "cultural" productions. Cultural policy is central to French government efforts to forge a strong sense of national identity.

In France, *culture* has become a kind of fetish, an object that stands on its own, outside of any human efforts to make it (van Beek 2000). It is often portrayed as a kind of wealth—the French term is *patrimoine culturel*—belonging to the French nation that can be catalogued and counted, much like real estate or jewelry. The objective of French cultural policy is to preserve and reproduce this *culture*. French national culture, however, has the added characteristic of being more than merely national. In the view of many in France and elsewhere, French culture—in the form of music, cuisine, art—is synonymous with civilization in general. Contemporary French composers do not write French music but contemporary music, and painters do not paint only French art. French high *culture* is understood in France to be universal *culture* (Bourdieu 1979, 1981).

One objective of French education and cultural policies since the nineteenth century has been to create a national understanding of French *culture* that serves as the basis of a coherent national identity. This effort often included the repression of local languages and folk cultures, replacing them with the French language and a Paris–approved literary and artistic canon. Often condemned as a form of imperialist racism when practiced in the colonies—including the French Antilles—these policies were exercised just as vigorously in the *métropole* in an effort to turn Basques, Bretons, and Corsicans, among others, into French citizens.

However, local cultures and their artifacts were not simply erased. At least since the establishment of the Musée des Arts et Traditions Populaires in the 1930s, local customs and traditions have been collected by ethnographers and folklorists to be documented and exposed as elements of folk cultures. These are incorporated into French national ideology as elements of a diverse past that contributed to the rich national cultural present (Cuisenier 1991). Instead of representing distinct national cultures that might challenge dominant ideas of what it means to be French, national cultural policy has worked to define regional cultures as folk cultures; subordinate parts of the national "high" culture.

The integration of millions of "Third World" immigrants into French society has created a similar challenge for French cultural policy. When the government liberalized laws regarding associations in 1981, allowing noncitizens to form and lead groups and receive subsidies, the governing socialists briefly flirted with the idea of multiculturalism. The principal agency involved with immigration policy, the Fonds d'action sociale pour les travailleurs immigrés et leurs familles (Social Action Fund for Immigrant Workers and their Families, FAS), along with the Ministry of Culture and local governments, began providing subsidies to associations that promoted immigrant cultures through the arts. The FAS only provided subsidies to groups with "foreign" origins, but the Agence nationale pour l'insertion et la promotion des travailleurs d'outre-Mer (ANT, or National Agency for the Promotion and Insertion of Workers from Overseas) provided similar assistance to Antillean groups in France. Since the mid-1980s, governments of both left and right have continued to subsidize immigrant associations, but they have concentrated on supporting groups that promote assimilation into French society (Blatt 1997; Hargreaves 1995). In the context of the reassertion of French republican cultural fundamentalism, immigrant representations of their *culture* must balance between a danger of being seen as completely foreign and unassimilable in French society, or merely minority folk cultures, subordinate to the national "high" culture. With their deep historic ties to France, this problem is especially acute for Antilleans.

As members of French society, Antilleans shared the French fetish for cultural representation. The choice to turn to the arts, *le culturel*, to express Antillean identity in France makes sense in this context. A way of life, a culture, was something one possessed. It could be identified by its expression as *le culturel*. Yet why represent the lives of Antilleans in the islands rather than in France? Why use theater? Why address a mostly Antillean audience?

FIGHTING ASSIMILATION

The decision to organize Eloge and to use theater as a tool to bring Antilleans into sharper cultural self-consciousness was not the result of a well-thought-out strategy. Rather, one Antillean in Paris wrote a play and turned to a group of friends to organize an amateur theater troupe that would produce his play. There are dozens of neighborhood cultural centers in Paris, funded by the French government and the municipality, where residents can exercise, attend classes and lectures, and arrange meetings for the groups they organize. Eloge met in one of these centers, a modern glass-and-steel box hemmed in on all sides by nineteenth-century buildings, a short walk from my apartment in the ninth *arrondissement*. The first rehearsal I attended, on a Friday evening in 1989, was somewhat jarring. A young woman, Claudette Henri, the group's theatrical director, told me that I was welcome to stay. But my presence raised questions. Should the actors carry on the rehearsal in Creole or should they speak French, given the presence of a "European"? I insisted that they not change anything for me and noted that I was not, in any case, a European. Everyone laughed at this comment and someone pointed out that the term "European" was used to avoid saying "white." Someone else added that maybe I was right. After all, they usually used "European" to refer to a French white person, and I was certainly not French (see Fig. 4.1).

Figure 4.1   Members of Eloge with the author, 1989.

Eloge was formally organized and registered as a 1901 law association with an elected president and other officers and a formal set of statutes. The association received small subsidies of a few thousand francs annually from the ANT, which it used to purchase scenery and meet other expenses involved in mounting a play. However, most of the funding came from membership dues and the fees other organizations paid for their performances. Its legal status gave Eloge legitimacy and allowed it to be listed in catalogs of Antillean associations. On paper, Eloge also had a formal purpose that went beyond theater. According to its statutes, it was a "group for the study of Antillean identity."

But the reality was not quite so formal. The core membership, about a dozen people, was Guadeloupan and related to one another through ramifying kinship ties. Claudette, for example, pointed out that four of the women and one of the men were cousins. Another member, Albert Christophe, told me that two of the current members as well as the man who wrote Eloge's initial play, were his cousins. A Martinican man who participated in the group had joined at the urging of his girlfriend, also a regular participant and one of Claudette's cousins. The only unrelated, non-Antillean regular was a white metropolitan Frenchman who was dating another of Claudette's cousins. Albert said to me, "We are a family affair."

Eloge was a working-class affair as well. None of its members had gone to university, although most had completed some vocational education beyond high school. The women, who made up more than half the core group,

Figure 4.2   Eloge relaxes.

worked predominantly in public sector jobs (e.g., as administrative assistants for the city or hospital aides), while the men were skilled workers in the building trades. Most lived in the working-class suburbs that ring Paris in comfortable but Spartan low-income housing projects. This mirrored the general profile of Antillean migrants in Paris. The youngest member was twenty-two, although most were in their late twenties. None were married, but one of the women was divorced and two had small children. With the exception of the white French member, everyone in Eloge had been raised in the Antilles—all first-generation immigrants who had come to France in their late teens and early twenties for work or job training.

Most members of the theater troupe had family in France outside the association—Claudette had four sisters living in the Paris region. Their personal migration stories followed the classic pattern—first living with siblings or other kin and then finding their own jobs and apartments. But that meant they often lived far across the city from their families. It was impossible to drop in for a visit, Claudette told me, as they had done in Guadeloupe and Martinique. They felt isolated in Paris.

This profile suggests that Eloge functioned to organize the social lives of a group of young unmarried Antilleans living in Paris. Rehearsals were often informal affairs with a great deal of time spent gossiping, discussing news of friends and family, and planning group outings. The group often met on weekends to celebrate someone's birthday. On those occasions, the women prepared Caribbean food, spicy Antillean *boudin* (blood sausage), for instance, followed by a *colombo de porc* (a pork curry), while the men brought Guadeloupan rum and cassettes of the latest *zouk* music. Members often went out dancing at Caribbean nightclubs. Most had family living in France, but Eloge was at the center of their social lives. Claudette remarked, "If I didn't have Eloge, I would be bored to death."

Isolation was accompanied by cultural alienation and loss. Claudette remarked that many Antilleans in metropolitan France were so concerned with fitting into French ways that they had lost their sense of identity. She wrote a poem berating Antillean women for adopting French women's ideas of beauty and failing to appreciate what was beautiful about themselves. Claudette's remarks inspired Eloge members to write a sketch in which a man walked around a seated woman, reciting the poem as an accusation. Although the text was written by a woman calling on other Guadeloupan women to be true to their own beauty and homeland, the subtext included women's fears that "their" men preferred French women.

Fear of assimilation arose partly out of experiences of racism and rejection in France. In May 1989, as France prepared to celebrate the bicentennial of the French Revolution, I joined Eloge for a weekend of rehearsals at a youth hostel in the town of Chartres. On the way to the train station at the end of the weekend, we encountered a parade of people carrying colorful flags, some dressed in strange uniforms. They were part of an annual celebration by French Catholics who had resisted the reforms of the Second Vatican Council, groups notorious for their association with the nationalist and xenophobic extreme right. This made many in Eloge uneasy. As we stood and watched the parade, we were handed a flyer from an organization calling itself the "Anti–89," in reference to the bicentennial of the 1789 revolution. The flyer called on all good and true Frenchmen to join the organizers on the following August 15 at the Place de la Concorde in Paris for a mass to expiate France's sin, committed two hundred years previously, of regicide. The particular terms used in the flyer to describe French history, for example, calling the Revolution an "unholy disruption," suggested that France had been ripped from its true path and identity and that only expiation could return it to its correct place in history.

The association between groups such as this Anti–89 and the extreme right, as well as their desire to eject all immigrants from France, made everyone uneasy. As one member told me, "It is at times like these that I do not feel at all French." It was becoming clear to me that most of the group members had experiences that left them feeling like outsiders in France much of the time. Claudette mentioned a radio discussion of the so-called aggressive nature of black people in France, which according to the commentator was part of the problem presented by "tribal" people living in France. This infuriated her, and in reaction she wrote a poem about the violent legacy of slavery and dispossession and the remarkable patience of Antilleans. One of the younger members, arriving at rehearsal in an agitated state, repeated the racist remarks a coworker had made about Antilleans. "I live in France," Claudette said, "but this is not my country."

France, with its chilly weather and raw climate of racism, was a foreign, cold place for Antilleans. Eloge performances evoked a lost world, life in Guadeloupe and Martinique. Antilleans came together at these events, sharing Caribbean food and dancing to *zouk*. In addition to making people nostalgic, the plays and poems were meant to help restore people to themselves, returning their Antillean *patrimoine culturel* and identities. Albert remarked that theater provided a way to "define who we are on our own terms."

The theater troupe rarely chose to portray Antillean lives in France. The few sketches of life in France they created—always in rehearsal, never in a public performance—focused on alienation and cultural confusion. In one sketch, an Antillean is mistaken for an African by a white Frenchman, while in another, an old Antillean woman in France, abandoned by her assimilated children and unable to return to the islands, prepares to commit suicide. I asked why they never performed these in public. "Nobody wants to see that," Claudette said. "Our plays should make up for the lack of warmth here, not remind people of it."

CREOLE CANTATA

The French fundamentalism about culture that Eloge members experienced had pushed many immigrants, including Antilleans, into a search for their own identities. Many ethnic activists turned to the arts to validate the existence of their own ethnic cultures. Other groups, such as the Antillean arts association known as Stand-Fast, shared neither Eloge's nostalgia for their islands of origin nor their philosophy of escapism in regard to the racial problems they faced in France.

Stand-Fast was organized around a semiprofessional collection of performers and artists (see Fig. 4.3). Its objective was to broaden the range of artistic styles associated with Caribbean *culture* in metropolitan France. Instead of reproducing traditional forms of music and art from the Antilles, Stand-Fast created a style of high art relevant to and embedded in the arts of contemporary France. In addition to performances, it developed workshops for aspiring musicians, actors, painters, and sculptors in which members of the association trained others in this new creolized style. They chose their name to reflect these objectives. "Stand-Fast" is an English translation of the Creole phrase *tchimbé rèd*, used when leaving friends. Using English pointed, I was told, toward the context of the entire Caribbean, to diasporic ties with Africa, West Indians in the United Kingdom, and African Americans, while giving the group a kind of cosmopolitan cachet lacking in other Antillean associations.[2]

Figure 4.3   Stand-Fast rehearses.

   Their first performance took place in a working-class, heavily immigrant neighborhood in Paris in a small theater seating about thirty people. They sat in old movie theater seats; the stage was an empty space in front of the seats. The only scenery was an old curtain at the back, behind which the performers waited for their cues. The audience, a mix of white French people and Antilleans, friends and family of Stand-Fast members, journalists and representatives of the Paris theater community, had received colorful, professionally printed invitations to the evening's event. Despite the simple setting, the well-dressed crowd made the evening more than a community event. Stand-Fast had professional ambitions.

   The show began with a burst of drum rhythms and dancers performing what the program referred to as African dance. From behind the curtain, the choir softly sang a verse of the folk song "Adieu Foulards," traditionally sung to departing sailors and to Martinicans and Guadeloupans leaving for France. Maryse Carbet entered from behind the curtain and recited the poem "Hiccups" by the Guyanese poet Léon Gontran Damas (1972, 38). The poem recounts the conflicts felt by a young Martinican, torn between his parents' insistence on proper French behavior and his own attraction to the life of working-class black children. The poem ends as the child is told by his mother that he must continue violin lessons because mixed-race children do not play banjo or guitar, instruments associated with the uncivilized elements of society. As Maryse finished, two guitarists entered, seated themselves on folding chairs without a word, and performed a classical composition derived from

Caribbean folk music. The instrument, subversive, non-French culture in the Damas poem, in the hands of a Caribbean musician, produced music that could be part of the French musical canon.

A complex drum solo followed the guitars as the choral group emerged from behind the curtain to sing a round in Creole, "Le Canon des Nègres Marrons" (The Round of the Maroons), which recounts an escaped slave's struggle for survival. Another poem honored resistance to slavery and the struggle against its reestablishment under Napoleon; it predicted yet another uprising of the population of Martinique, who would destroy the statue of the Empress Joséphine in the main square of Fort-de-France. The choir sang an homage to the revolutionary leader of Haiti, Toussaint Louverture. This "stage cantata" began with the song "Adieu Foulards" and then evoked the exile and imprisonment of Louverture in France.

In the final scene, drummers played a fast, complex rhythm as a man stepped forward to sing a *damier*, a Martinican chant that accompanies simulated combat between two male dancers. This was accompanied by the reading of a fictional account of a *damier* from a Creoliste novel by Raphaël Confiant (1988, 165). At the end of the *damier*, the singing group began a rhythmic chant while fashion models strolled across the stage, wearing clothes designed by a member of Stand-Fast. A final flourish from the drums ended the performance and the audience erupted with applause and cries of "bravo!"

A Caribbean Aesthetic in France

That this was *culture*, there could be no doubt. All the trappings were there: the theater, music, dance, art. But what sort of *culture* and, more importantly, whose? The performance was clearly grounded in the Caribbean, drawing on the story of Toussaint Louverture and sung in Creole, with powerful drum rhythms moving everything along. But the poetry, recited in elegant French, recalled the conflicts at the heart of Antillean identity, torn between Europe, Africa, and the Caribbean. Classical guitar music, with its subtle, entrancing rhythms, was not something people associated with the heavily produced dance music common to Caribbean nightclubs and radio programs. How and why did the fashion show that concluded the evening fit? If *le culturel* is the best way to express a way of life, whose way of life did this performance represent?

These were precisely the kinds of questions that Stand-Fast organizers hoped to raise with audiences. I had heard that the group was working to develop representations of Antillean culture in France that were less "folkloric" than groups like Eloge. I began to attend the group's evening rehearsals and soon found myself doing more than observing. At the first rehearsal I attended, the group's musical director, Michel Toussaint, asked if I could sing. "We need more male voices," he observed, since females outnumbered males four to one.

I had doubts about my musical abilities but soon found myself singing bass. A week later I paid my dues and became a member of the association.

Like Eloge, Stand-Fast met once or twice a week for rehearsals often lasting two or even three hours. They involved intense work, singing scales and then repeating the parts of the *Canon des nègres marrons* over and over until the choir director was satisfied. If few of the participants were professional singers, many worked or hoped to work in the arts. Michel, for instance, was a composer and classically trained guitarist, as was his wife. Maryse Carbet was pursuing an acting career. Jean-Pierre Clément, the group's main organizer, was a professional photographer and his wife was a clothing designer. Stand-Fast included journalists, musicians, painters, designers, and university students. There were few kin ties between members. Instead, they had met through mutual friends, at festivals, at parties, or through work.

The participants in Stand-Fast were relatively well educated. Most had or were working on university degrees. Although they were raised and often continued to live in the same suburbs as Eloge members, participants in Stand-Fast were more likely to come from middle-class families; they had parents who worked as government administrators, engineers, lawyers, and ministers. A few were first-generation immigrants from Martinique, Guadeloupe, or Haiti, but the majority of Antillean participants had been born and raised in France. They had little experience of life in the Antilles and were for the most part not Creole speakers. The group also included at least four white women, born and raised in France. Some were there because of relationships with Antilleans and others because of their interest in music and dance. All had formal training as singers or dancers and viewed Stand-Fast as an opportunity to develop as performers.

Like the metropolitan French participants, the Antillean members felt that working with Stand-Fast would give them valuable performance experience, which was hard for Antilleans to obtain because French directors often pigeonholed them. Maryse, for instance, said that she was too white to be cast as an Antillean or African but too black for white roles. At best, she was cast as an exotic prostitute or island temptress. Michel said he could produce popular electronic Caribbean music and gain fame if not fortune, but as a classical musician with Caribbean roots, he had no audience.

Just as they felt miscast and misunderstood in the world of French arts, however, they were equally uncomfortable with the ideas of Antillean *culture* current in France. Jean-Pierre claimed that Antillean values are "falsified" in metropolitan France, reduced to a commercialized set of stereotypes focused on a mythical tie to the islands. The representation of Antillean *culture* in France, he added, is reduced to "*boudin, rhum, et zouk*" (i.e., spicy Antillean sausage, rum, and popular dance music). Black people in general and Antilleans in particular are seen through what he termed *doudouiste* stereotypes, which emphasized a kind of tropical sensuality and exoticism. This was evident, Jean-Pierre commented, with the topless black women who danced along one of the floats in the 1989 bicentennial Bastille Day parade. The French do not respect our way of life, he added, noting that no Antilleans had any say in how they were represented in the parade. French art producers acted as if Antilleans were incapable of speaking for themselves or creating their own image. They failed to recognize the accomplished professionals in the Antillean community. Our best leaders have always been ignored and disrespected in France, he told me, adding that "Gaston Monnerville," born in French Guiana and long the leader of the French senate, "should have been president of the Republic" instead of de Gaulle.

Yet Jean-Pierre and others in the group thought that the responsibility for this lack of respect lay with Antilleans in France, not the French. "Ours has not been a proper immigration," he told me, adding that "proper" immigrant groups "colonize" the country in which they settle, first preserving their own integrity by living together in a well-defined neighborhood and establishing their own institutions, then making their own ways of doing things a part of the traditions of the broader society. Antilleans have never had their own neighborhoods in France and have done little to make their own institutions. Isolated among the French, they are overwhelmed by metropolitan values and rapidly lose any sense of identity. Another member pointed to the success of *zouk* music in France—its commercial success, she said, undermined efforts to revive or appreciate traditional music forms from the Caribbean.

The "second-generation" children of immigrants in Stand-Fast had somewhat different concerns. Maryse, for instance, often remarked that even after her visits to Martinique, she could not consider herself entirely Martinican. There were important differences, she told me, between the way people lived in the Antilles and our way of life here in France. Another member told me that she wanted to create art that reflected her experiences as an Antillean born and raised in France. A graduate student, she came from an activist family. Her father, an immigrant from Martinique, worked in the Paris subway and had long been active in the Communist trade union and Antillean associations. She had traveled to the Antilles several times but, she told me, "I am not recognized as a Martinican when I go over there." In France, however, representations of Antilleans were entirely controlled by French people. "They produce the images of who we are," she said, "and that is not right."

Group members from the second generation saw racism in France as a direct result of having an ill-defined *culture*. Because the French do not know who we are, one said, they disrespect us. It is not sufficient to fight racism by joining groups like SOS Racisme, she noted. Such groups denounce specific instances of discrimination and lobby for better laws against racism, but they do not promote understanding. They cannot, she added, because they are broad coalitions, representing all the groups subject to racism in France. Hardly anyone knew that the leader of SOS Racisme, Harlem Désir, was Martinican.

"Everyone is there," she said, meaning that every ethnic group was represented, "but nobody can find themselves there." Members of Stand-Fast were great admirers of African Americans in the arts because, Maryse told me, they had succeeded in representing their own lives in ways that went beyond stereotypes. After a group of us went to see Spike Lee's 1989 film *Do the Right Thing*, Maryse commented that "we will be better off when we can make movies like this ourselves" in France.

Reviving Antillean traditions was not Stand-Fast's main objective. While members wanted to maintain a connection with the Antilles, they were concerned with forging a sense of identity for the "second generation," who had been raised in France. If the first generation had failed to make a "proper" immigration, the second was alienated from their parents' origins, with few real ties to the islands their parents came from, Jean-Pierre said. Our objective is to rescue them from this "zoukified" alienation and show them that Antilleans in France can make real art. This required, he added, creating audiences among both Antilleans and French people who are capable of appreciating what we are doing.

Jean-Pierre and Michel wrote out statutes for the group that defined Stand-Fast as a "research group for a Caribbean aesthetic." "This means," Jean-Pierre said, "that we are not limited to reproducing an idea of the *culture* of the Antilles and that we can experiment with creating arts that represented a Caribbean sensibility in metropolitan France." Stand-Fast would be avant-garde and its work, organizers hoped, would be recognized as the kind of "high art" associated with French *culture*, rather than regional folk art. While reproducing "traditional" Antillean art forms played a role in Stand-Fast performances (that was the role of the *damier* in the performance described above), tradition took a backseat to experimentation and mixture. Drummers wore African clothes and the fashion show was designed around the diverse people the designer saw on the streets of Paris. Performances incorporated music and poetry from Martinique and Guadeloupe, history from Haiti, and African rhythms. Jean-Pierre told me that they intended to broaden their reach, to include material from the Hispanic and Anglophone Caribbean. If the Stand-Fast aesthetic was grounded in the French Antilles, it was built on the cosmopolitan sensibilities of Antilleans living in metropolitan France. Rooted in the Caribbean but built on the experiences of the second generation, Stand-Fast expected to transform French culture.

ENGAGING *CULTURE*, TRANSFORMING CULTURE

The genius of the French nation, as policymakers and intellectuals see it, lies in the nature of the *patrimoine culturel*. It incorporates—or subordinates, depending on one's point of view—the regional cultures in the country, turning them into folklore. French culture is national but also universal, held up around the world (or so French culture professionals fervently hope) as an example of civilization. Everyone should want to be French.

Antilleans in France, however, want to assert their identity through the representation of their own *patrimoine culturel*. As French citizens, they are expected to assimilate the goals and values of the Republic, to see themselves in the rhetoric and representations of French policy and culture makers. Antilleans understand—or are expected to understand—that the public assertion of difference is an illegitimate political act in France, one that places them outside the national culture. Assertions of difference threaten to undermine the unity of the Republic. Unless, of course, it is the Republic's representatives who legitimize cultural difference. Antilleans have already been designated as culturally different in this manner by people like the mayor who claim to respect their culture even as they critique its manifestations. Others view Antilleans as representatives of "tribal" cultures, perpetually dancing to the beat of a liberating drum. Finding a way toward asserting their difference while navigating between these and other stereotypes is no simple matter.

Eloge uses nostalgia for life in the Antilles to build a sense of identity and community. Drawing on members' experiences with racism and their feelings of not belonging, the theater troupe's performances call on Antilleans to remember who they are by looking to the place from which they come. They turn their back on definitions of Antilleans in French national culture, placing themselves instead as members of a distinct society across the Atlantic. Eloge had little difficulty finding enthusiastic Antillean audiences for its plays. It created a distinct social world for its members and connected their activities to a broader Antillean community in the Paris region. Their performances reminded their friends and relatives of their cultures of origin, thus holding off assimilation for the duration of the performance. Yet with little hope of returning permanently to the Antilles, Eloge's performances provided few resources to help Antilleans make sense of their place in French society.

Members of Stand-Fast would have dismissed Eloge as amateurs performing in the service of myth making. Pushed, like the members of Eloge, to think about their own identity in France, they came to a different conclusion. Instead of turning toward the Antilles, they claimed a place within French society. They asserted their right to define their participation in that society and the terms of their contribution to France's *patrimoine culturel*. They worked to make their contribution fit within the world of the French avant-garde. Stand-Fast drew on so-called high art forms—classical music, dance, fashion, painting—that are central to French high culture. They incorporated a Caribbean aesthetic into those forms, drawing attention to the distinct elements of diversity within French society. Stand-Fast could not count on Antillean nostalgia or on Antillean youth and their taste for pop culture. Rather than rely on kinship networks and friends, Stand-Fast focused on building a professional base for its art.

Faced with the broken promise of cultural assimilation, Antilleans in France are struggling to define their place in French society. They experiment, sometimes turning with longing toward the Antilles, at other times to their cold, sometimes hostile adopted country to negotiate the terms of their acceptance. The rise of hip-hop during the 1990s has complicated this process, as many young musicians from immigration's second and third generation—including many Antilleans—have drawn on global forms of music to carve out a space and identity within French *culture*. French rap has drawn mostly on the experiences of life in the working-class and immigrant suburbs of the big cities. But it has also turned nostalgically to the Caribbean, claiming its roots in Martinique and Guadeloupe.[3] This combination of global *culture*, the gritty life of the suburbs, and Antillean nostalgia may be a first step toward redefining France in multicultural terms.

Notes

1. See Chapter 1 for more details regarding the discussion with the mayor.

2. Stand-Fast is a pseudonym, but it reflects the group's real name, also in English.

3. Bruno Beausire, the Paris born hip-hop artist known as Doc Gynéco, has made the Antilles a focus of his work. See, for instance, his album *Première consultation* (1997), especially the song "Né Ici," and *Solitaire* (2002), especially "West Indies."

Further Reading

Gilroy, Paul. 1993. *The Black Atlantic: Modernity and Double Consciousness.* Cambridge: Harvard University Press. This book links the work of several black intellectuals with the development of the arts, especially music, in the African diaspora, raising critical questions about resistance to European domination and the creation of new forms of culture.

Hargreaves, Alec G., and Mark McKinney, eds. 1997. *Post-Colonial Cultures in France.* London: Routledge. A collection of essays focusing on representations of immigrants in the arts and the media in France, as well as on the ways in which immigrant communities there have used the medias.

Murray, David A. B. 2002. *Opacity: Gender, Sexuality, Race, and the "Problem" of Identity in Martinique.* New York: Peter Lang. An analysis of how *culture* and the making of "cultural citizens" have become central to political life in Martinique, with a particular focus on gender, sexuality, and performance.

Price, Richard, and Sally Price. 1997. "Shadowboxing in the Mangrove." *Cultural Anthropology* 12, no. 1: 3–36. In this critical analysis of cultural politics and activism in the French Antilles, the authors raise useful questions about how Martinican and Guadeloupan intellectuals use culture in political activism.

CHAPTER FIVE

CAN MAGIC FIX A
BROKEN CULTURE?

CHAINS IN OUR HEADS

In February 1989, I attended a continuing education seminar for social workers who often encountered Antilleans in their practice. The course took place at the Université Paris Nord in the working-class suburb of Villetaneuse, one of many universities constructed in the years following the rapid growth of the student population in the 1960s. Jean Galap, a psychologist and president of the Centre d'entraide et d'étude des antillais, guyanais, réunionnais (Center for Solidarity and Study of Antilleans, Guyanese, and Réunion Islanders, CEDAGR), had invited me to the seminar, part of a series he had organized that year.

Galap began the class by challenging the students to identify him. Was he an Antillean? He resembles the stereotype of the academic, impeccably if somewhat conservatively attired, pipe in hand and a slightly ironic twinkle in his eyes. The consensus around the table was that Galap did not look like one. Light-skinned with short hair and a neatly trimmed beard, he could be, as he said, a *métèque quelconque,* any sort of foreigner. Because he does not have a stereotypical "phenotype" or an identifiable Antillean accent, he is not often identified as Martinican. This is true, he added, for many Antilleans. The first lesson for anyone who wants to understand Antilleans in France, he concluded, is that you should not rely on visible markers like skin color to identify them.

Then Galap asked the ten students seated at the conference table to introduce themselves and explain their experiences in what he called "intercultural relations." There were two students from Guadeloupe, three from Cameroon, and one each from Mauritania, Cape Verde, Algeria, Morocco, and France. This initiated a lively exchange. The student from Mauritania said that her mother was Senegalese, so that intercultural relations were built into her family. She confessed to a certain prejudice against Antilleans who, she said, seem alienated from their "true African culture." Antilleans strive to be European, she asserted, but Europe is not really their culture. A Cameroonian student suggested that she get to know Antilleans better before passing judgment on them. His older brother, he noted, lived with an Antillean woman and she hardly seemed culturally alienated to him. The lone French student seemed almost apologetic for his lack of international background or colorful family. He said that he believed, by way of apology, that one of his ancestors had been an Italian immigrant. At the end of the introductions, Galap noted his disappointment with the small number of French people present. Intercultural relations, he remarked, should not be a concern only for minorities.

The Moroccan student asked if a person or group could maintain a distinct cultural identity while remaining "open to others." The capacity to deal with other groups is variable, Galap answered, and is rooted in the strength of a group's ethnic identity. Ethnicity is a way of recognizing who you belong with, of knowing who is in the same group as you. In general, he continued, there are at least seven indicators of ethnicity: a common territory, similar physical characteristics, the same native language, a common folk culture, shared religion, similar political views, and shared economic activities. Moroccans, he commented, seem to have a sufficiently "well-anchored" identity to know who they are while dealing with other groups. But Antilleans—using himself as an example—have an ambiguous and undefined identity. Many of us are unsure of who belongs in our group and we do not share a common vision of the world, he added.

Galap described a study of housing discrimination in which he had participated. The researchers wanted to see if landlords would discriminate among potential renters on the basis of ethnicity. They chose three men with similar education, middle-class job, and family situation to look for apartments in the Paris region. One was a white Frenchman, another was a Portuguese immigrant, and the third was Guadeloupan. Seven landlords offered an apartment to the white Frenchman and five were willing to rent to the Portuguese man; only one was willing to lease an apartment to the Guadeloupan. This experiment, Galap added, reflects the experiences of many Antilleans in France.

Perhaps we can overcome ethnic or cultural differences by pointing people toward human universals, one of the students suggested. Galap dismissed such "metacultural" ideologies. They are most often asserted by members of the dominant society, he said, who want to erase ethnic differences and impose their own culture in the name of the "universal." The history of the population of the French Antilles, in which slavery and colonial domination are central, has led to a kind of cultural mixture, a *métissage* that is both artistically productive and psychologically problematic. Antilleans' inability to clearly define their status vis-à-vis France, he said, is indicative of the problems this cultural situation has created. In metropolitan France, Antilleans are confronted on a daily basis with the need to define themselves as either French or not French, but they are ill-prepared to make that choice. Even after being confronted with racism, most Antilleans are quite happy when French people tell them that "you are just like us." Antilleans want very badly to be French, he said, even when French people will not accept them.

Drawing on experts in family and kinship, education, magic and religion, and economics, he explained that the seminar would provide students with insights into the range of areas in which Antillean and French cultures clash, often at the expense of the former. Understanding these experiences would help the social workers in their relations with Antilleans. One of the Guadeloupan students commented that a cultural approach to social work was especially necessary with Antillean clients. Antilleans cannot learn to deal with any idea of the universal, or the metacultural, before they are secure in their own identity, he said, adding that "we still suffer from the alienation of slavery and our dependence on France has left chains in our heads."

SOCIAL POLICY AND IMMIGRANT CULTURES

The idea that social workers and policymakers should strengthen the cultural identity of immigrants is a radical idea in France. In the United States, by contrast, social policy is often fashioned in ways that are meant to take cultural differences into account. In France, since the end of the nineteenth century, social policy has been based on the assumption that the nation must be represented as both culturally homogeneous and structurally diverse. The policies at the core of the modern welfare state in France have been designed around social class, not ethnicity. *Le social* is a term used in France to describe areas in which government policies are required to reduce the structural tensions brought on by class differences and ensure "equilibrium" in society. Policies concerning health, workplace safety, retirement, unemployment, child care, and family support are designed around the fundamental goal of maintaining social solidarity and reducing the possibility of class conflict. These policies are most often negotiated with the leaders of workers unions and employers associations, referred to as "representative institutions" and "social partners." This focus on social class, justified by social science, served through most of the twentieth century as a means to legitimize government social policies and reduce class tensions (Donzelot 1994; Horne 2002).

Immigration since World War II appears to challenge the idea that social policies should not be modified for culturally distinct groups in France. In the view of some French political leaders and social service providers, if immigrants have not "adapted" to French society, it is because they have not "adopted" French culture. The job of service providers, from this perspective, is to enforce French manners of thought and behavior (Grillo 1985; Hargreaves 1995). The culture of the migrant is significant only because it is not French. Some service providers believe that immigrant groups carry whole cultures in their heads—cultures that cannot be transformed or abandoned, traditional cultures that are incompatible with French society. Their children—whether they choose to become French citizens or not—are similarly trapped in their foreignness. At best, immigrants and their offspring can be described as existing "between two cultures," condemned to remain out of place. The most policymakers can do is manage and control cultural differences. This view has led to the assertion by politicians, public housing managers, and some service providers, that a kind of "threshold of tolerance" exists in neighborhoods, a percentage of the immigrant population beyond which conflicts will arise that will drive out white French residents and lead to the establishment of ethnic ghettos. This has resulted in the implementation of quotas limiting access to low- and moderate-income housing in some cities in France. Illegal but tolerated, such quotas are often applied to "foreign" immigrants as well as Antilleans and justified as a way of maintaining the "French character" of housing and neighborhoods.

Efforts in the 1970s and 1980s to develop policies to fit immigrants into class-based social policies opened the door to those who would make demands in the name of cultural difference. In the 1970s, the French government developed various programs to preserve links between immigrants and their home countries. They provided space for religious services in low-income housing projects and worker hostels and hired language instructors for the children of immigrants. These programs were created, usually in association with the governments of sending countries, with the idea that such policies would facilitate the repatriation of immigrants. But the implementation of such policies demonstrated that policymakers recognized that immigrant groups had needs that could only be addressed through policies oriented toward their distinct cultural origins (Hargreaves 1995, 203–204).

Recognition of immigrant cultural differences became more explicit in the 1980s. In 1981, the socialist-led government liberalized laws regarding freedom of association, allowing noncitizens to form and lead associations. The government agency most directly involved with addressing immigrant needs, the Fonds d'action sociale pour les travailleurs immigrés et leurs familles (Social Action Fund for Immigrant Workers and Their Families, FAS), which had mostly focused on housing policy, began to subsidize immigrant associations. By 1991, the FAS was subsidizing more than 4,000 associations.[1] These subsidies went mostly to groups that promoted the adoption of French values by immigrants (Hargreaves 1995, 205). Recognizing that immigrants and their children were unlikely to "return" to their countries of origin, governments in the 1990s developed policies in education and urban development that were designed to integrate immigrants into French society by teaching them French values. Using the FAS and other agencies, French governments have increased their reliance on private nonprofit associations to carry out these policies (Ullman 1998; Ragi 1998; Wihtol de Wenden and Leveau 2001; cf. Pelissier 2001). While in the 1990s, both left- and right-wing governments promoted policies designed to teach immigrants and their children to adopt French republican values, their reliance on immigrant associations and the subsidies furnished to them resulted in a proliferation of those associations.

Antilleans are also able to take advantage of the French state's increased reliance on nonprofit associations in the administration of social policy. The Agence nationale pour l'insertion et la promotion des travailleurs d'outremer (ANT, or National Agency for the Promotion and Insertion of Workers from Overseas), the Ministry of Justice, the Ministry of Culture, and the Ministry of Education, as well as local governments, have made funds available to associations that promote the "insertion" of Antilleans into French society. However, Antillean associations, like other immigrant organizations, have had to formulate their actions in ways that reflect the priorities of French policymakers (cf. Galap 1987; Pastel 1987). While Antillean and other immigrant activists have worked to make *le culturel* central to policy, promoting their own groups as new "social partners," French policies have continued to subordinate *le culturel* to *le social*. Galap's course was designed around these distinct objectives.

Making the Case for Culture

Before becoming a psychologist, Galap was a Catholic priest, a career he chose because he thought the Church would provide a useful platform for social activism. Working as a priest, first in France and later in Martinique, he realized the limitations on his ability to be an effective agent of social change. The Church allows you to engage in humanitarian action, he told me, but not to address fundamental social and political issues. He left the priesthood and became a psychologist, thinking that psychology would provide tools he needed to understand and act on the problems Antilleans like him faced. But psychology led him to academia, where he met some of the same limitations on his actions he had encountered in the Church. Organizing the CEDAGR was one way to transcend those limitations.

The seminars featured guest lecturers from the CEDAGR. The association was designed as a "relay" or formal connection between the government and Antilleans in France. Founded in 1977, the CEDAGR's core membership of approximately twenty-five people—social scientists, social workers, journalists, government bureaucrats, and university students—were predominantly first-generation migrants from the Antilles. Their advanced degrees gave them legitimacy as "concrete intellectuals" who study, comment on, and formulate social policy in France (Foucault 1981, 304; cf. Kauppi 1996). Several had written books and articles focusing on aspects of Antillean life in France; the group published a short-lived scholarly journal entitled *Mawon: Les cahiers de l'immigration guadeloupéenne, guyanaise, martiniquaise et réunionnaise*, as well. Conceived as a combination think tank and advocacy group, the association represented, Galap told me, the scientific voice of the Antillean migration in France.

The CEDAGR worked in a wide variety of ways to assert Antillean specificity in France, for instance, establishing a lending library specialized in the French overseas departments and territories and migration, the only library of this sort open to the public in Paris. The group reached out to Antillean university students, helping them adjust to life in France and assisting them with research projects that focused on the French Antilles or migration. Association members frequently gave public lectures, spoke on radio programs, and helped organize a variety of events at universities and cultural centers. They worked hard to make a case for public recognition of Antillean distinctiveness in France, most often coupled with an analysis of what they called the "psychosocial cost of nonrecognition."

This perspective was most obvious in the work of Hélène Migerel, a Guadeloupan psychoanalyst and CEDAGR member who specialized in religion and magic practices among Antillean migrants in France. Migerel presented her research in one of the seminars organized by Galap.[2] He introduced her talk by pointing out that other specialists in France often dismissed magic as not belonging with the study of religion, which led them to misunderstand a fundamental part of Antillean culture. Since Antilleans are predominantly Catholic, religion was theoretically not a barrier to their adaptation to life in France. But Caribbean magical beliefs and practices, which French people often associate with Haitian Vodou, marked Antilleans as different.

Migerel began by discussing the origins of Antillean magic practices. Born of the encounter between Europeans and Africans in the sixteenth century, Antillean magic owes as much to the beliefs of rural Bretons who migrated to the Antilles as to those of kidnapped Africans who became slaves. She pointed out that sixteenth-century Europeans were as likely to believe in magic as Africans. In the Caribbean, the African slaves observed and eventually adopted—were forced to adopt—Catholicism, but they reinterpreted the Catholic rituals and saints in their own terms. In the process, they created their own religious practices and reinvented the magical beliefs and practices of Africa and Europe, shaping them to meet their own needs. She noted, however, that it would be a mistake to define Antillean magic as a religion distinct from Catholicism.

Magic in the Antilles is an extension of the Catholicism practiced by the majority of Antilleans, not an alternative.

Migerel distinguished between white and black magic and their respective practitioners, carefully noting the different names and activities ascribed to each in Guadeloupe and Martinique. The landscape of the Antilles is enchanted, she explained, noting the association between particular places, beliefs, and practices. Although magic is usually associated with rural and relatively poor Antilleans, she suggested it is also part of the intellectual life of urban Antilleans, including those of greater economic means. While not all residents of the islands believe in magic or consult with practitioners, everyone is aware of the practice. It is a central part of life in Martinique and Guadeloupe, she added, and the island cultures cannot be understood without taking it into consideration.

Magic in the Antilles has a negative side, in Migerel's analysis. This is rooted, she said, in the "Antillean personality," characterized by an inability to assume responsibility for one's actions and a tendency to blame others for misfortune. The refusal of the Catholic Church to recognize and sanction the interaction between Antilleans and local magic practitioners creates a sense of guilt among Antilleans who are involved in magic. Because of this, Antilleans are obsessed with the hidden activities of others but are unable to speak openly about their problems and are unable to take effective action themselves. Only a practitioner of magic can help. Although magic is an essential part of Antillean culture, Migerel concluded, it poses a psychological danger for individuals.

The Paris landscape is not enchanted in the same way. Antilleans who migrate to France must find alternative sites of meaningful spirituality—the tomb of nineteenth-century spiritist Alain Kardec in Père Lachaise cemetery or the chapel on the Rue du Bac where the Virgin Mary visited the novice Catherine Labouré in 1830. Similarly, magic practitioners who serve Antilleans in Paris must also adapt to the new setting. They keep their practice similar to that in the Antilles, since those who consult them need the evocation of their homeland. In Paris many of the products used in magic prescriptions are difficult to acquire, and consequently many ingredients have been changed to locally available materials. In Guadeloupe, she noted, the *saints*—the term refers to the spirits that possess some practitioners—speak French, but in France they speak Creole. This suggests that in France magic works to restore links to home for Antilleans.

In the Antilles magic is used to guide business decisions, resolve affairs of the heart, and address health issues. The same, Migerel observed, is true in France. At a sociological level, magical practices can be used to repair social relations between Antilleans; on a psychological level, to relieve tensions and control aggression. But in France these practices can no longer fulfill their promise. Antilleans in France work and live with French people who do not use Antillean magic. They may dismiss belief in magic as mere superstition, a sign that Antilleans are not quite "civilized." In this context, Migerel claimed, using magic can engender feelings of guilt, an overly fatalistic attitude toward life events, or an aggressive reaction to misfortune.

Turning to magic has cultural costs in France as well. The order of preference in selecting a consultant, according to Migerel, goes from the Antillean *gadézafé* to the French *voyant* and only after that to the African *marabout*. This is evidence that Antilleans suffer from "deculturation," an inability to identify what is closest to their culture, and indicates, she added, that Antilleans do not have a "normal" relationship with their own culture in France. The Antillean ideal is European and anything associated with Africa is seen as bad. In metropolitan France, such factors as a white majority and the devalorization of African culture reinforce this dichotomy in favor of European values, causing Antilleans to suffer "cultural trauma."

Migerel reminded students that for most Antilleans, migration is a potentially traumatic experience. Expecting to be accepted as French, they instead find themselves rejected as foreign. They frequently experience housing discrimination, find their upward mobility blocked at work, and are treated as foreigners by the French. Magic as they used it in the Caribbean does not address these difficulties. Worse, French social workers often respond to reports of magic practices as if they were signs of mental illness.

Addressing this situation would require, Migerel concluded, serious attention from the government. She proposed three steps. First, organizations that work with Antilleans, including social service agencies, schools, and employers, should be made aware of the reasons Antillean migrants turn to magic. They should be taught to see that turn as a logical step in Antillean cultural terms, when confronted with the traumatic experiences of migration. Second, whenever possible, Antillean therapists should be brought in to work with Antillean clients. They would be less likely, she said, to evaluate the use of magic as a sign of mental illness and would be better prepared to treat the client in a culturally appropriate manner. Finally, efforts should be made to teach Antillean migrants about resources other than magic that are available to help them overcome the stress and tension of migration. From legal action against discrimination to ethnic activism, Antilleans would learn the cultural tools available to address their problems in France.

TURNING TO THE STATE

The CEDAGR was designed to help Antilleans learn to address the difficulties they faced as immigrants. The series of continuing education seminars for social workers it organized was one way of accomplishing that objective. The intention was to present a series focusing exclusively on Antillean migrants. However, the agencies that provide funding for Antillean initiatives (e.g., the

ANT) were unwilling to provide enough money for the CEDAGR to act alone. The FAS had funds but would finance the seminars only if they also focused on "foreign" immigrants; Antilleans were not sufficiently "foreign" for that agency.

Galap and his colleagues had convinced associations representing other immigrant groups of the value of such seminars and organized a broad series focusing on intercultural relations. But Galap told me that he found the government's failure to understand that Antilleans merited specific attention and their lack of recognition for Antillean cultural specificities frustrating. He noted that government bureaucrats generously funded programs for other immigrants but denied grants to the CEDAGR on the grounds that "you Antilleans don't really have any problems here; after all, you are French."

In addition to advanced degrees and research experience, the CEDAGR membership was well connected in government agencies and the Antillean community. Some members worked at the ANT, at the Ministry for Overseas Departments and Territories, and in other key government agencies. Elected officials from the Antilles attended the association's annual general meeting, demonstrating close connections across the Atlantic as well as in the *métropole*. In addition, CEDAGR members were active in other Antillean associations, providing links to a wide array of Antillean activists. The CEDAGR could represent itself as a group of reliable experts and professionals, capable of the detachment required for policy research and social services that groups devoted to advocacy usually lacked.

Establishing that legitimacy with government agencies and other Antilleans required walking a fine line between advocacy and scientific detachment. The CEDAGR held monthly meetings in offices it rented in a middle-class apartment complex in Paris. Meetings often included discussions of how to manage this tension. Their budget depended largely on grants and contracts from government agencies, and by the mid-1980s, conservative governments had reduced funding for the cultural training services that the CEDAGR provided. The organization had difficulty—even with its contacts—competing for and winning the contracts it needed. When the political climate changed in the late 1980s and early 1990s, more funding became available. Some members felt that closer ties with political parties could help reduce the impact of changing political priorities. But such ties could also damage the association's reputation for independence. "It must be clear," one member asserted, "that we do not 'roll' for any political party."

Although members agreed with the goal of political independence, each grant or application revived the debate. The Ministry of Justice had asked the CEDAGR, for instance, to provide training for court workers who dealt with young Antillean men and women designated as "at risk" (*en pré-délinquance*). One member, a Guadeloupan social worker in his mid-thirties, noted that it would make more sense for the association to provide counseling directly to the young Antilleans. But the government did not consider Antilleans to be sufficiently distinct to require the services of other "natives" of the Antilles. Others agreed with this analysis of government priorities, adding that there were plenty of contracts for other immigrant groups, often involving the use of native social workers. "We don't scare the government enough," the social worker said, adding that "we are neither Kanaks nor Corsicans . . . maybe we need to shock them a little before they will help us out," referring to clashes between French police and Kanak separatists in New Caledonia and Corsican separatists in Corsica.

Another member, a psychology student from Guadeloupe in her midtwenties, argued that Antilleans would not be taken seriously until they were seen to be a coherent, well-organized community in France. This, Galap pointed out, is precisely why we have to avoid any specific political affiliations; "our position is that we have to be taken seriously as Martinicans and Guadeloupans, which transcends political cleavages." It is true, the student responded, that our demands to be understood as Antilleans should be seen as transcending French political differences. Perhaps we can avoid being identified with any political parties, but we cannot really escape politics, she added, because "our demand for recognition is inherently political in France." This insight into the political nature of their demand for cultural recognition in France led her, she later told me, to decide to return to Guadeloupe as soon as she finished her degree. She thought that recognition would only come, as it had for Algerians, when Guadeloupe became its own nation, completely independent from France.

CULTURE AND DISASTER

Student members of the CEDAGR decided to put together an exhibition focusing on natural disasters in the French overseas departments. The exhibition, entitled *Rain, Wind, and Fire,* featured meteorological and geological explanations for the volcanic eruptions, earthquakes, and hurricanes that threatened life and property. It also provided an opportunity to critique French colonial policies and inspire visitors to think about how Antillean identities were grounded in a territory and history substantially different from that of metropolitan France. The organizers secretly hoped that the exhibit would inspire French viewers to rethink their ideas about tropical paradise and develop a new respect for Antillean specificity.

Planning for the exhibition was interrupted by a real disaster. On September 17–18, 1989, Hurricane Hugo severely damaged parts of Guadeloupe. Reactions in metropolitan France were swift; the government mobilized rescue operations, sending troops, material assistance, and high-level officials within hours of the storm's passing. The emigrant community mobilized rapidly and many Antillean associations contributed to the effort. CEDAGR members had watched the approaching storm carefully and, drawing on their government contacts, stayed informed about the extent of the disaster.

The first formal posthurricane CEDAGR meeting took place two days after Hugo hit Guadeloupe. Searching for some way to assist their compatriots, many people who rarely participated in the association's activities crowded the meeting. Much of the first meeting, however, was devoted to debating the association's relationship with other Antillean groups involved in providing assistance. A group of prominent Antilleans in Paris, for example, had decided to form an umbrella organization called Guadeloupe Solidarité to coordinate the efforts of the community and to prepare long-term development plans for the island. The group had no legal status, having decided not to take the bureaucratic steps necessary to create a formal association. Members wanted instead to establish themselves as a pressure group, working to ensure that the reconstruction of Guadeloupe, by the French government, was guided by the needs and interests of Guadeloupans, not the priorities of the French state. Other efforts to organize assistance were also reviewed, including public and private initiatives.

The CEDAGR had been invited to join Guadeloupe Solidarité but viewed it and some other Antillean efforts to coordinate assistance with suspicion. Given the large number of groups raising money, collecting goods, and hiring shipping containers to send the goods to Guadeloupe, the CEDAGR's role was still uncertain. One CEDAGR member suggested that the leaders of these efforts were taking advantage of the disaster to gain power and influence with the government. Could this undermine the ability of the CEDAGR to function as a "relay" for the government in other contexts? We have to do something, Galap argued, or people in France will think that Antilleans are incapable of helping themselves. Concurring with this, another member pointed out that the Antilles were already seen as depending entirely on France and its welfare state. What is more important to us, he asked rhetorically, to be important Antilleans in France or to show solidarity with Guadeloupe? Whatever we do, he insisted, we must avoid reinforcing the image of Antilleans with their hands out for help.

In the end, members decided to develop a few targeted actions that would reflect the CEDAGR's larger concerns with culture and psychological adaptation. Drawing on their insider knowledge of events in the government and their access to news sources in both France and Guadeloupe, they established a telephone information line. Antilleans in France would be able to call and get instructions on where to make donations, on the latest damage assessments, and on actions they could take as individuals. They would also use their contacts in the media to get invited on radio programs where they could provide information on the CEDAGR's actions. As the situation developed, the CEDAGR would work out other ways of providing assistance.

The next day Guadeloupe Solidarité held a press conference to announce its objectives. Meeting in an elegant salon at the Ministry for Overseas Departments and Territories, there could be no doubt that the organizers of Guadeloupe Solidarité were at least as well connected to the government as the CEDAGR. The group was represented by several prominent leaders in the Antillean community in France, including a lawyer, a well-known television journalist, an actor, an association president, and a demographer from the French national statistical agency. The latter outlined their concerns and objectives. They could, he said, rely on the French government to provide a great deal of material assistance. But the hurricane damaged a society that was already faced with severe problems, he added, and Guadeloupe Solidarité wanted to make sure that reconstruction did not merely return the island to its previous status. Its objective was to help rebuild Guadeloupe physically by helping restructure local institutions. We need to draw, he added, on local government, the private sector, and resources from the European Union, making ties that help Guadeloupe outgrow its dependence on the French government.

The association president, a well-known activist in the governing socialist party, remarked that he was a Guadeloupan first and a socialist second. This government, as well as past governments, he said, has failed to develop a productive economy in Guadeloupe, leaving us practically incapable of dealing with disasters like Hugo. "I saw a newspaper headline today that announced 'France coming to the aid of its devastated island,'" he noted, "and it made me want to laugh." The island has been devastated for a long time, he added, and we must push the government to do more than rebuild. Guadeloupe must be developed into a genuinely productive economy.

Just as he finished, the minister for overseas departments and territories, Louis Le Pensec, a tall, elegantly dressed white man, strolled into the salon, flanked by several aides. Given the disaster in Guadeloupe, Antillean members of press were visibly surprised when he reminded the audience that he was the government spokesman as well as minister and spent several minutes outlining the details of budget discussions, focusing in particular on housing policy in France. He then turned to the topic of Guadeloupe, reviewing in detail the damage and explaining the measures the government had decided to take. Metropolitan France will show, he said, that it is not indifferent to the situation in Guadeloupe. The president of the Republic has said that we will make the reconstruction of Guadeloupe a priority, he announced. Le Pensec then changed the topic, discussing some other issues from the ministers council. His report made, he left as swiftly as he entered, leaving a somewhat stunned silence in his wake.

A few days later, the CEDAGR held another meeting. Hearing of the Guadeloupe Solidarité press conference, Galap said this confirmed his belief that the group was too close to the government. The CEDAGR should try to reach out directly to local governments and associations in Guadeloupe on its own, he said. Another CEDAGR member, a journalist who had attended the press conference, said it was clear from Le Pensec's presentation that the government was not making the disaster its top priority. He added that he had seen a report about the hurricane damage on French television the night before that demonstrated the incapacity of the French to understand what had happened. The report, he explained, had mostly focused on the destruction of tourist areas and the distress of European tourists. Although there had been some attention to the plight of locals, the French journalists seemed concerned that the hurricane had devastated a tropical playground. He pointed out that a similar disaster in France—an oil spill on the Breton coast, for instance—would be taken far more seriously, with investigations into the economic consequences for local fisherman and farmers and demands for large amounts of assistance. The CEDAGR decided to pursue its own initiatives, independent of Guadeloupe Solidarité.

A few weeks after the hurricane struck, Galap and Migerel went on Radio Beur, a station organized primarily by the descendants of North African immigrants, to discuss the disaster. Galap introduced the CEDAGR, explaining that their main objective had been the development of means to treat the psychological problems of the Antillean community in France. He added that as an activist as well as an academic specializing in immigration, he was aware of the suffering migrations impose on all the minority communities in France and thus was particularly grateful to Radio Beur for inviting Antillean groups to the program.

He then explained the CEDAGR's initiatives in hurricane recovery, aid, and assistance for Guadeloupe. Although there were important material needs in Guadeloupe, other groups were better equipped to respond to them. The bulk of the CEDAGR's work would focus on the island's long-term needs. Migerel added that the CEDAGR would work to address the psychological distress of Antilleans in metropolitan France by informing them about the ways in which disaster victims develop psychological mechanisms to maintain their will to survive in the face of catastrophes. They had also decided to organize a campaign for Guadeloupan children, asking children in France to send drawings to the mayors of the more devastated towns in Guadeloupe, to be distributed by them to children in their towns. This, she claimed, would work to eliminate feelings of abandonment among the victims of the hurricane. They hoped, she added, that this initiative would also help French children better understand the origins of Antilleans they might know in France, thus building intercommunity contacts. The CEDAGR was also working with a group of teachers to arrange assistance for the schools in Guadeloupe. They were collecting school supplies to be sent to Guadeloupe and arranging housing in France for groups of Guadeloupan students who would be coming there to study while they waited for their schools to be repaired.

Late in October, the CEDAGR organized a fundraiser to benefit Guadeloupan schools. Members drew on their academic and government contacts to put together an event that contrasted sharply with the style of the press conference held by Guadeloupe Solidarité. The setting was the Amphithéatre Durkheim, a lecture hall in the Sorbonne. A representative of the ministry for overseas departments and territories had been invited to brief the audience on the latest developments in Guadeloupe. But the evening's featured speakers were the minister for youth and sports, Roger Bambuck (a Guadeloupan), and the president of the Guadeloupan conseil général, Dominique Larifla. Musical interludes provided by *zouk* musicians lent an unusual atmosphere for a Sorbonne lecture hall. Money was raised from ticket sales, sales of the group's publications, and arts and crafts made by Antilleans.

The CEDAGR's fundraiser was a lively affair in a setting that drew government representatives out from the trappings of their ministries. The audience had no fear of asking sharp questions of government representatives. Roger Bambuck spoke as a Guadeloupan rather than a government minister, denouncing what he called the "colonial ideology" that saw Antilleans as incapable of shaping their own destiny. He called for greater solidarity between Antilleans in France and those in the Caribbean to demonstrate the error of the colonial point of view. He demanded that the dignity of Antilleans be respected.

The event was in all respects a success. The CEDAGR brought together a substantial number of Antilleans, raised money for Guadeloupe, and demonstrated its ability to draw on government officials in both France and the Caribbean. It had done this without compromising its image as an independent organization. Whether or not members had demonstrated the distinctiveness of Antillean societies was, of course, open to question. But as we left, one of the student members smiled and remarked, "*Zouk* at the Sorbonne! Who would have thought it possible?"

CULTURAL RECOGNITION, CULTURAL DISTRESS

In 1998, I visited Jean Galap at his office, deep inside the massive building that houses the medical school of the Université René Descartes in central Paris, where he updated me on the work of building recognition for Antillean specificity in France. The 150th anniversary of the abolition of slavery and the participation of Antillean players in the French World Cup victory provided a context, I thought, that would lead to greater recognition for Antilleans in France. But the mood in France had shifted again, he said. Policymakers had begun to emphasize "integration." They wanted to make immigrants—including Antilleans—into French people and reduce any cultural differences to private, individual practice. For Galap, "integration" was a code word for assimilation.

Integration policies were focused on those who suffered from "social exclusion," he explained, including unemployed people, homeless people, and even people with mental illnesses. Among these were unemployed suburban youth, mostly of immigrant origin, whose lives were characterized as *la galère* (the struggle), a term used to describe the generally distressed conditions of life many faced (Dubet 1987). Immigration had become incorporated in the national policy debates on poverty and social exclusion. This might be a form of integration, but it also meant that poverty was in the process of being racialized by association with immigrants. These developments had complicated efforts by those, like the CEDAGR, who wanted recognition for Antillean specificity in France. The children of Antillean migrants were being lost in *la galère* of national indifference.

Yet groups like the CEDAGR had succeeded in changing one aspect of French social policies. The French model for the welfare state had long understood society as being fundamentally divided by social class. Government social policy was organized primarily around the need to address the inequalities of class to the exclusion of all other social differences. Activists in the Antillean community, along with other immigrant activists, demonstrated the need for policymakers to attend to the *le culturel* as a source of social division in France. They had also succeeded in becoming "relays" between policymakers and immigrant populations. While political leaders in France may promote republican fundamentalism in their speeches, they have increasingly relied on nonprofit associations to represent and to provide services to immigrants and their children.

Notes

1. In 2002, the FAS became the Fonds d'action et de soutien pour l'intégration et la lutte contre les discriminations, the Action Fund for the Promotion of Integration and the Struggle Against Discrimination (FASILD).

2. She has also written extensively on the topic. See Migerel 1987, 1989. For a similar psychological approach to Antillean culture in metropolitan France by another member of the CEDAGR, see Lirus 1979.

Further Reading

Hyatt, Susan Brin. 1997. "Poverty in a 'Post-Welfare' Landscape: Tenant Management Policies, Self-Governance and the Democratization of Knowledge in Great Britain." In Cris Shore and Susan Wright, eds., *Anthropology of Policy: Critical Perspectives on Governance and Power,* 217–238. New York: Routledge. This analysis of the transformation of "the social" under neoliberal government policies and tenant activism in the United Kingdom suggests that the context for forming government policies has shifted toward local associations all over Europe.

Ireland, Patrick. 1994. *The Policy Challenge of Ethnic Diversity: Immigrant Politics in France and Switzerland.* Cambridge: Harvard University Press. A comparative analysis, from a political science perspective, of immigrant activism and its impact on government policy in France and Switzerland.

Ullman, Claire F. 1998. *The Welfare State's Other Crisis: Explaining the New Partnership Between Nonprofit Organizations and the State in France.* Bloomington: Indiana University Press. A study of how and why the French government has come to rely on nonprofit private associations for the development and implementation of social policies in the past few decades.

CHAPTER SIX

IN THIS WORLD, BUT NOT OF IT

CRY OF MEN, CALL OF GOD

Once a year, usually in October, the Aumônerie Catholique Antilles-Guyane de Paris (the Antillean and Guyanese Catholic Center in Paris) organizes a mass for the Antillean community. Led by a bishop from Guadeloupe or Martinique, the annual mass is one of the largest Antillean Catholic events in the Paris region, drawing over a thousand participants. In 1989, Bishop Ernest Cabo of Guadeloupe celebrated the mass at the Eglise du St. Esprit in central Paris. The church, a large red-brick structure, stands out sharply in a neighborhood of apartment towers. Built in the 1930s in honor of Catholic missionaries sent to evangelize the colonies, the church became the center of Antillean Catholic life in France for one afternoon.

People had begun to gather between two and three o'clock in the afternoon, expecting to enter the church and begin the mass. Instead, Antillean Catholic lay activists—members of parish-based groups from the Paris region—directed them to sites in and around the church where others from their home parishes were gathering. A group of people I knew from the suburb of St. Denis invited me to accompany them to meet with a group from their parish in the church basement. As we waited for someone to explain what to do, it became apparent that most of those present, despite living in the same parish or town, had not met before.

Several priests, all white Frenchmen, arrived and explained our assignment to the entirely Antillean and predominantly female crowd gathered in the basement. We were to spend an hour in discussion with fellow parishioners prior to the mass. We were told that our discussion should center on the theme *cri des hommes, appel de Dieu* (cry of men, call of God) and on a text from the Gospel of Matthew (25:34–40) in which Jesus asserts that doing good for others is a way of honoring him. Our discussion was led by two white French priests.

We asked each other, To whom should charity be extended? Should Antilleans direct their solidarity toward other Antilleans or toward everyone in France? One man asserted that Antilleans ought to give priority to helping other Antilleans. "Nobody pays any attention to us," he remarked, "we can only depend on ourselves." "But as Christians, we cannot discriminate among people," responded a young woman. A priest added that in extending charity beyond Antilleans, they would be building ties with other communities. This could prove difficult, another woman noted, since it is sometimes hard to understand where our neighbors come from. She told of being robbed by young men—probably immigrants, she noted—in her neighborhood. Others responded to this with more anecdotes about the difficulties involved in understanding their diverse neighbors in St. Denis, some recounting unexpected acts of charity and friendship, others telling of theft and vandalism.

Later we reunited with the other parish groups in the vast church sanctuary and sang Creole hymns accompanied by guitar and organ. Two dozen priests gathered at the altar, along with the Guadeloupan bishop. Except for the bishop and two others, all the priests were white. Representatives of each parish group came forward and recounted some of the conclusions reached during the discussions. One group called for greater solidarity with workers who struggled for better and more dignified working conditions. Another saw God calling parents to make a better world for their children, free from drugs, racism, and delinquency. Yet another asked for greater solidarity among the faithful so that they could aid each other in facing the challenges of life. Others gave examples of individual struggles in jobs or other activities, offering only prayer as an answer.

The bishop's sermon, interrupted by singing and praying, was in French, shot through with comments, jokes, and prayers in Creole. Focusing on the assigned scripture, he referred to the recent hurricane in Guadeloupe, suggesting that the destruction could be seen as a call from God for Guadeloupans, especially Christians, to construct a better society. Several times during the sermon he asked the congregation to pray with him in Creole, *Bondyé kouté nou, kouté pitit a'w, ou ban nou la vi mé nou bizwen fòs pou nou ay pilwen* (Hear our prayer, Lord, listen to your children. You have given us life, but we need strength to go further). Bishop Cabo ended his sermon with a traditional Creole salutation: *Tchimbé rèd, pa moli* (Stand firm, do not give up).

Many congregants lined up to receive the sacraments from the bishop. Then we joined hands and sang a last Creole hymn, "Bay lanmen, sé fwe aw" (Join hands, here are your brothers). A crowd gathered around the bishop, seeking his blessing, while others stopped to greet friends. Slowly everyone dispersed into the streets, chatting animatedly. "That was wonderful," commented an activist from St. Denis as we left the church, adding that she hoped more people would feel encouraged to join lay groups in their parishes now. "If we can create warmth in the Church here in France," she said, "the Church can once again serve as a center for Antillean life."

Religion, Ethnicity, and the French State

Antilleans are overwhelmingly Catholic and the Church plays a central role in many people's lives (Lacroix 1989). It is not surprising, then, that some Antilleans in France would work to make the Catholic Church central to their efforts to organize an Antillean community there. However, making religion central to ethnic identity also challenges the secular ideology that is one of the core values of the French Republic. Conflicts over the role of the Catholic Church in public life are central to the historical development of this ideology. Since the 1980s, however, the preservation of the secular nature of French public life has become an important issue in debates about the integration of immigrants into French society.

Since the Catholic Church has historically provided the basis for a political identity distinct from and resistant to the Republic, the separation of church and state in France has been defined primarily by a desire to prevent the intervention of the Catholic Church—or any other religion—in the secular affairs of the state. While freedom of religion is guaranteed for individuals, practice of a religion is expected to be a strictly private affair. This means that the expression of political views from a religious perspective is theoretically illegitimate. Religion should not play any role in the relationship between the individual citizen and government. In addition, while religious organizations are free to regulate their own internal affairs, each is kept within the officially defined realm of religion through careful state oversight. In France, Catholics, Protestants, and Jews have so-called representative organizations that maintain ties with the Ministry of the Interior. One of the main objectives of government policies in the 1990s was to establish a similar representative organization for Muslims.

While there have been many exceptions to the ideology of secularism in France over the past century—early public school closings once a week to allow students to attend catechism, for instance—policymakers and cultural critics have asserted, in the context of debates about immigration, that maintaining the secular purity of public life in France is central to the survival of the Republic. Conflicts over the balance between religion and secularity have come to stand for race and ethnicity in France and are used to attack the legitimacy of the political actions of immigrants in French public life. For instance, a 1996 issue of the weekly French newsmagazine *Le Nouvel Observateur* featured a series of articles under the headline "What Muslims in France Want."[1] The lead article argued that it was difficult to make sense of Islam as a religion in French terms. The growth of Islam in France, the article asserted, represents a cultural rather than religious problem. The tendency of Muslims to confound categories, such as religion and politics, was illustrated by a photo showing Muslim men praying in a makeshift space in a Renault factory. From the point of view presented in these articles, for Islam to become an unambiguous religious phenomenon—and a French one as well—would require substantial changes in the beliefs and practices of Muslims in France. The failure to make this transformation, it would seem, is what keeps North Africans and their descendants in France in the status of "immigrants"— living in France but never becoming French.

Around the same time, another weekly news magazine, *Le Point*, featured a series of articles under the headline "The Protestants' Revenge."[2] Once the object of savage repression, Protestants in France have quietly succeeded in becoming deeply embedded in French society. As the articles made clear, Protestants are French, and they practice a specifically French brand of Protestantism. An editorial writer noted that Protestants are a religious minority ("interesting but not worrisome") that has made significant contributions to the national community.[3] Protestantism, he asserted, corresponds with the hopes and aspirations of large numbers of French people because it promotes both individual responsibility and social solidarity. Unlike Islam, Protestantism does not challenge French secular traditions. It represents, according to these articles, precisely what religion is supposed to be in France. Photos accompanying the articles showed well-dressed groups of white men and women praying in their churches or working in comfortable government offices. They clearly understand, the photos implied, how to separate religion, politics, and work in France.

Despite the putative limits on its political action imposed by secular ideology, the Catholic Church has long been involved in social activism in France. A Catholic trade union, Confédération française de travailleurs chrétiens (CFTC, French Confederation of Christian Workers), was formed in the 1920s, and the Church has long organized young people through a variety of associations such as the Jeunesses ouvrières chrétiennes (JOC, Young Christian Workers). In the 1950s, the Church deployed "worker priests" who shared the living conditions of industrial workers and worked to transform the idea that the Church belonged exclusively to the bourgeoisie. These organizations, known collectively as Action Catholique, served to demonstrate that the Church could also be responsive to the interests of the French masses and not just the elites. Church organizations continue to play a significant role in social policy, lobbying the government for assistance and working as a relay for state agencies. The political opinions of Catholic officials on public policy are carefully reported in the media and the religious motivations of intellectuals, union officials, and even some politicians are recognized and accepted.

The place of the Catholic Church in contemporary France is profoundly ambiguous, caught between demands that it adjust doctrines and policies to the lifestyles of the French and demands that it provide a base for those who reject those lifestyles. It is portrayed alternatively as the representative of the forces of unenlightened reaction, as well as a source for leftist and New Age ideologies. This ambiguity reflects on most other religions in France, since the Catholic Church is the quintessential representative of religion there; when French people use the term "Christian" what they usually mean is Catholic. Although each group has its particular history in France, Protestants, Jews, or Muslims must operate from within general French ideas about the place of religion in society, as well as ideas about people who practice any sort of religion. Given their long attachment to France, Antilleans are more aware of these constraints than other immigrants.

ANTILLEAN CATHOLICS IN A FRENCH CHURCH

Seven months before the community-wide mass, I attended a two-day retreat with about sixty Antillean Catholic activists at a convent in the Paris suburb of Coubron, led by Father Pierre Lacroix. In his welcome speech, Father Lacroix, a Guadeloupan priest and chaplain of the Aumonerie, noted that the Aumonerie was an ethnic mission, created to serve the spiritual needs of Antilleans in France. But the mission needed to do more than preserve Antillean ties with the Church, he said. At the retreat, the lay leaders—this was the fourth annual meeting of the group—were to work on creating new reasons for Antilleans to see the Church as a source for identification and social action in France.

At the first meeting three years before, the group had focused on the kinds of problems Antilleans in the Church in France faced, seeking reasons to develop an ethnic community within the Church. The second annual retreat had examined the attraction between Antilleans in France and other religions, especially Protestant groups like Seventh-Day Adventists and Jehovah's Witnesses. The third year they had discussed the growing importance of lay activists in the Church. Following this review of previous retreats, Father Lacroix asked representatives of each parish to report on their activities over the previous year.

A leader from St. Denis said that they had been able to bring Antillean Catholic traditions to their parish—a New Year's Day mass, for example. This tradition of offering the New Year to Jesus, she said, had long brought Antilleans into the Church in the islands and succeeded in St. Denis as well. In addition, she noted, although Antilleans were key organizers of the mass, many non-Antilleans participated as well. They had also organized a service around the stations of the cross on Good Friday that had been well attended, as well as services for children, Bible studies, and other activities. Creole singing and Antillean practices had been incorporated in most of these, she added. She reported that French church members had received Antillean activism in the parish well. They said Antilleans had "breathed new life" into the parish.

Other parishes reported similar success in organizing church events with Antillean themes. Antilleans were likely to come to church for other specific holidays, especially All Saints Day. In addition to holidays, groups reported success in organizing weekly or monthly Antillean masses. If we include singing in Creole, one man said, and hold a reception after mass, we can create "warmth," a church atmosphere that makes Antilleans feel welcome. Another group reported that Martinicans and Guadeloupans were receptive to special catechism classes, groups organized around themes like parenting, preparation for baptism, and other life events that are practiced differently in the Antilles than in France. One parish reported that they had also recruited a large group for a pilgrimage to Lourdes and suggested that such organized outings were especially popular with Antilleans.

Yet others reported problems. Several group efforts met resistance from clergy and other parishioners. In one parish, efforts to organize an Antillean group to pray the rosary had been forced by the priest to move out of the church; they met instead at a parishioner's home. The priest felt that the Antillean character of the group would drive away other church members. Perhaps, an older woman commented, the priests are afraid that they will lose authority to Antillean lay activists if they allow too much obvious ethnic organizing. A priest attending the meeting agreed, noting that he had assigned one of his colleagues, a priest who had spent several years working in Guadeloupe, to reach out to the Antillean community in his suburban Paris parish. Father Lacroix noted that the Portuguese immigrant community in Paris had succeeded in building their community around masses in their own language. Yet they too were limited in what they could accomplish in building an ethnic movement within French churches. In France, he said, church leaders did not want congregations to become identified with one ethnic group.

Many Antilleans were not active in the Catholic Church. "Antilleans want to come to Church to see a performance, they want to attend a well-performed mass," one activist reported, "but they do not want to be responsible for organizing the mass themselves." Some Antilleans fear coming to church, Father Lacroix remarked, because their lives are not in order. They are living with partners to whom they are not married, for instance, and fear what the priest might say. Another man pointed out that life in France is antireligious, and consequently "it is difficult for us to live our faith openly here." This drives Antilleans away from the Catholic Church and, he added, into less visible religious practices.

Our goal, as both Christians and Antilleans, Lacroix told the group, is to form a community. To be a Christian requires engagement in community building, he said. To be an individualist concerned only with your own soul is a form of heresy. Jesus, he reminded them, used a net to fish, not a line. All our sacraments, from baptism to the Eucharist, are celebrated together. You cannot even be alone with God when you pray, he joked. You are always in a group of four: yourself and the Holy Trinity. Our goal is to build community solidarity, first among Antilleans and then with the broader Christian community. To do this, we must make our churches warm and welcoming places, as in the Antilles, places where we listen to the concerns people bring from the rest of their lives. But we also have to reach out to people in their other activities—be active in politics and unions and in other Antillean associations, including the Aumonerie. But, he concluded, I am expecting you to keep working as missionaries, to overcome the solitude experienced by Antilleans in France by making the Church a place for community building in this country.

CREOLIZING THE FRENCH CHURCH

Catholicism defines religious life in Martinique and Guadeloupe. However, for most Antillean Catholic activists, the Catholic Church is more than the majority religion. As they describe it, the Church in the Antilles is an institution into which Antilleans are born and in which they play an unquestioning part. As labor leaders and educators, Catholic authorities play important roles in nonreligious life in the Antilles. The Church occupies a far more central place in the Antilles than in contemporary metropolitan France. As one priest in Guadeloupe told me, when asked about the significance of Protestant churches there, "they are a club, but we are society."

It is this centrality of the Church in Antillean social life that Catholic activists would like to reestablish in metropolitan France. Antillean ties to the Church remain strong, activists believe, but they remain rooted in the Caribbean. This may be quite literal, as one priest told me, since Antilleans often return to their home parish in Martinique or Guadeloupe for major rites of passage such as a First Communion. For first-generation migrants, the Church is intimately linked to the neighborhood or town in which they were raised; parishioners are both family and friends. These social ties are absent from churches in France.

Just as there are no Antillean neighborhoods in the Paris region, there are no Antillean parishes in metropolitan France. The Aumônerie Antilles-Guyane, led by Father Lacroix, serves as an ethnic mission. Located in central Paris, the Aumônerie provides space for activist meetings of all sorts—the CEDAGR met

there before finding its own offices. It is the center for organizing a broad network of Antillean Catholic activists in France. Lacroix had attended seminary
with the CEDAGR's founder, Jean Galap. From a deeply Catholic family, with
one brother a priest in Guadeloupe, Lacroix believed strongly in the Church's
capacity for social action. As chaplain to the Antillean population in France, he
hosted a weekly radio program on a private Antillean radio station, attended
masses organized by lay groups around the city, organized meetings at the Aumonerie, and attended many of the secular events organized by other associations. He also published and wrote articles for a widely read bimonthly
magazine, *Alizés*, which focused on both secular and religious matters that confronted Antilleans living in metropolitan France. Lacroix also worked as a liai-
son between French Catholic authorities and Antilleans, reaching out to parish
priests to tell them of the particular needs and practices of their Antillean
parishioners. Without specific efforts to include them in the Church, he said,
Antilleans fall away from practice or, worse, turn toward other religions. They
tell him that the Church in France is cold and unwelcoming.

"Antilleans do not trust the Church in France," he said. They have developed an anticlericalism distinct from that usually found in France, rooted in
a perception of the Church as allied with interests that have historically ex-
ploited Antilleans, of being primarily a white, French Church. They see the
Church hierarchy as powerful in both religious and secular terms. Priests are
thought to possess secret knowledge and power that they keep from ordinary
people and their commitment to morality is suspect.

The religious practices of Antilleans present obstacles to framing communities within the Church in metropolitan France. Antilleans practice an individualist brand of Catholicism, Lacroix said. They emphasize appeals to
saints, individual devotions, pilgrimages, and the purchase of masses over the
regular attendance of community-wide masses on Sundays. They resort to
Antillean magic and consult with its practitioners. French Catholic priests see
these practices as deviant, bordering on idolatry, which makes them suspicious of their Antillean parishioners. When they encountered Antillean demands they thought were related to magic, Lacroix encouraged parish priests
to send them to him instead of denouncing the practices. "I don't feel any
special vocation for providing this service," he said, "but at least I know what
to expect and can avoid driving Antilleans from the Church."

The primary goal of Lacroix's outreach work is to organize Antillean lay
groups in each parish, groups meant to make Antillean migrants feel "at
home" in metropolitan French churches by organizing the teaching of catechism, pilgrimages, and other activities that metropolitan French churches
either do not provide or do not provide in a way that meets Antillean expectations. At the same time, however, these groups provide leadership experiences for the Antillean laity in the Church. They form a network that

stretches across the Paris region, contributing leadership and structure to Antillean activism both inside and outside the Church.

The relationship Father Lacroix would like Antillean Catholic lay activists to develop starts with the "Kingdom of God" and a recognition of the significance of human communities. Salvation comes through social life, he said, through collective activities and experiences. In the case of Antilleans, it is necessary to examine problems of migration and settlement in France. It means adapting the Church's message to different cultural groups in order to bring them to salvation since, as Lacroix notes, individual experience is determined not only by social class but by cultural identity as well.

Lacroix and the other Catholic activists want to place the Church at the center of Antillean identity, as a central institution around which the community can organize. They reject both the Antillean view that the Church is primarily a dispensary for certain spiritual services and the French idea that the Church should confine itself to the realm of private belief. Instead, they work to emphasize the idea that the Church is a social space for communal solidarity and understanding of social problems. Instead of focusing on repentance for individual sins, Lacroix found the "signs of Jesus' victory" in the development of agape, or "fraternal communion," defined as a search for respect of diversity and the sharing of resources and responsibilities.

Two factors limited these theological goals. First, a respect for and interest in diversity should not lead Antilleans too far away from the community of the "universal Church," so Lacroix and the other activists do not intend to form their own ethnic parish. Instead, their strategy emphasizes a creolization of metropolitan French parishes, allowing the concerns as well as the creativity of Antilleans to influence the form of the Church in France. At the same time, they expect to transform the religious practices of Antilleans by building on Caribbean practices, developing new religious references, including less dependence on clergy and a more engaged and active laity. These "new religious references," as one activist called them, are to be constructed around one fundamental ideal: an ethnic and spiritual community.

LEAVING BABYLON

Several hundred Antilleans gathered together every week in Paris for services in the Seventh-Day Adventist Church. In the early 1990s, there were fifteen Adventist churches in the Paris region, all but two serving largely Antillean congregations. Unlike the Catholic activists, the Adventists have made no effort to define themselves as Antillean; there is little in their religious practices to distinguish them from non-Antillean Adventists in France or anywhere else.

Adventists observe the Sabbath on Saturday, and members of the church gather for the weekly Sabbath service at nine o'clock in the morning. One church I attended was located in central Paris, hidden from the street in a courtyard, in what looked like a renovated warehouse or factory. The church was sparsely decorated, with rows of wooden pews and kneelers facing a broad platform on which the pastor and some of the elders sat. Following Adventist custom, there were no crosses on display; the only decorations were fresh flowers on the ends of the platform and a citation from Isaiah 35:4 on the wall, "Prenez courage, ne craignez point; voici votre Dieu . . . " ("Be strong, fear not! Behold, your God . . . ").

The main sanctuary held approximately six hundred people with overflow seating on balconies and in another room where people could watch the service on a video monitor. Congregants come with their families from all over the Paris region. Few live anywhere near the church; they must rise early on Saturdays in order to dress and arrive on time. But this does not dissuade them and it is usually necessary to arrive early to get a seat in the main sanctuary. The Saturday Sabbath begins with Bible study called "Sabbath school" before the formal church service. Shortly after nine o'clock, with a precision unusual for secular Antillean gatherings, the congregation sings a few hymns and then splits into small discussion groups; regular participants usually sit in the same place each week, near other members of their Bible study groups. Led by one of their members—the position rotates annually—the group discusses a portion of the Bible that they studied at home during the preceding week. Their studies are guided by a pamphlet called the *questionnaire*, which is published in the United States and translated into French. Adventist churches all over the world use the same pamphlets at the same time. As one Adventist explained to me, it is possible to go to a church anywhere in the world and keep up with one's Bible studies because each congregation will be studying the same passages at the same time.

Seventh-Day Adventist Bible study focuses mostly on eschatology. I participated in the Sabbath school with a group of seven others, led by a Bernard Lambert, a Guadeloupan in his mid-forties. On the September Saturday I will describe here, our discussion focused on Revelation 17 and 18. These chapters describe a vision of a woman sitting atop a beast that has seven heads and ten horns. The *questionnaire* provided us with a basic analysis. The beast represented Satan and his partisans on earth, while the woman represented a confederation of churches centered on the Catholic Church that chose to follow Satan and tie themselves to earthly powers. The reading described the destruction of the woman, called "Babylon," and the suffering of her followers in the end times. While our study guide explained much of the imagery, our task was to decide the implications these chapters held for our daily lives. Bernard, who was also a church elder, guided us toward their meaning. To follow God, we decided, we needed to "go out of Babylon" by rejecting worldly values. Leaving behind worldly things, Bernard indicated, was what made Adventists the "spiritual Israel," God's people.

A bell rang from the pulpit, signaling the end of our discussion. Another church elder, one of the Sabbath school organizers, reviewed the lesson from the pulpit and a soloist performed a hymn—in French. Then the elder read a verse from the Gospel of Matthew, the same verse on charity that had been discussed during the Catholic mass described above. The Adventist interpretation, however, asserted the necessity of making contributions to the church's endowment fund. The Sabbath school ended with the reading of one last Bible verse, calling for the redemption of God's people, and the singing of hymns.

Following community announcements—reminders to reduce noise in the courtyard outside the church and requests for housing for visitors—the service began. The pastors and some of the church elders entered the church and took their places. The pastors at this church, as in most Adventist churches in France in 1989, were white Frenchmen. Nearly all the other church officials, elders and deacons, however, were Antilleans. An elder read a Bible verse to the congregation and then led them in prayer. Next, deacons passed through the congregation collecting tithes and offerings for the church.

One of the pastors delivered a sermon about how church members should prepare for the new year—in France, the beginning of the school year each fall, *la rentrée,* is the occasion for reflections on the coming year for adults as well as children. How, he asked, will each person contribute to building the church of God in the coming year? Each member must bring an individual spiritual light to the church. Each must contribute to the mission of the church, to the "harvesting of souls," he said, citing John 4:35. Telling the story of Jesus offering water to a Samaritan, he says that "we must reach out to everyone, regardless of origins." Adventists must speak of their certitude that Jesus is Christ to all people; they must be more aggressive in witnessing to others about their personal experiences with Jesus. He reminds the members that most had come to the church because they heard this message from a friend, a family member, or a coworker.

At the end of the service the congregation followed the pastors, elders, and deacons into the hall and courtyard. Members split into small groups, chatting animatedly, greeting friends, and exchanging news of the week. Even in this less formal setting, conversations were mostly in French rather than Creole. After an hour or so, the crowd dispersed, most returning home for lunch. For some, the afternoon would be devoted to activities in the church—committee meetings, Bible studies, youth groups—while others went on "missions," often taking the Adventist message door-to-door in the neighborhood of the church.

Public Adventists, Private Antilleans

A Guadeloupan journalist I knew asked me to explain why, if I was interested in Martinican and Guadeloupan activists in metropolitan France, I spent so much time with the Seventh-Day Adventists. Growing up in Guadeloupe, she explained, she thought that Adventist children were snobbish and aloof, purposefully separating themselves from other children and inspiring a good deal of resentment. They were not representative of Antillean society—either in the Antilles or in France (Massé 1978). When we attended an Adventist service together, she sat quietly, looking a bit bewildered by the whole affair. Later, however, she told me that during the service she felt as if she were in a Guadeloupan village. But she expressed surprise at the possibility that Antilleans could be happy in the atmosphere of the Adventist church. After all, she said, they forbid all of those things that we do to remind ourselves of who we are. They don't drink rum, they don't listen to *zouk* music, and they rarely speak Creole.

Here is the paradox of the Seventh-Day Adventists in Paris. Although they are an Antillean church in terms of membership, their behavior and ideologies mark them as Adventists first. As a majority in the Seventh-Day Adventist Church in Paris, Antilleans have made the church into an Antillean space, but that fact is secondary to Adventist identity. Within the broader context of metropolitan French society, their objective is to make their identity as Adventists of primary significance. Their Antillean identity becomes private and secondary. In the latter, at least, they are also following the logic of French assimilationist ideology.

Bernard invited me to his apartment for lunch one Saturday after church. He lived with his wife, son, and a boarder, an Adventist from Guadeloupe, in a modest apartment in a housing complex in a working-class neighborhood of Paris. In gestures and language, Bernard presented himself as an Adventist who merely happened to be Antillean. We stopped to pray as we entered the apartment and prayed again before we ate. The apartment was large, bright, and simply decorated, with a large map of Guadeloupe on one wall and a shelf of dolls dressed in traditional Antillean clothing. The tablecloth and napkins were decorated with maps of Martinique. As we ate a simple meal of cold salads, quiche, and fruit juice, Bernard told me that he would prefer to live in Guadeloupe but would not be able to find work there. Throughout the meal, he was more interested in explaining the meaning of being Adventist then in talking about being a Guadeloupan in France.

Raised in an Adventist family in Guadeloupe, he had been baptized in his early teens. Adventists do not practice infant baptism, he told me, because joining the church is a choice. Seeking work, he had emigrated to France in his early twenties and entered the building trade with help from other church members. He believed in living an exemplary life to demonstrate to others the benefits of being an Adventist. This meant, he explained, that he did not drink or smoke, that he was a good worker, and that he would not join unions or political parties. Those are, he said, worldly things.

Other church members also explained that Adventists should reject the world. "We are in this world, but not of it," they said. For Adventists, the material world is the site of an enormous conflict between the forces of God and the forces of Satan. The development of this conflict can be followed, they said, through close examination of biblical prophecies, especially those found in the Old Testament book of Daniel and the New Testament book of Revelation. Adventists view these prophecies as a sort of history of the world, explaining the past and predicting the future. As they see it, the world is currently experiencing the end times, and the second coming of Jesus is imminent.

These true followers are, for the most part, assembled within the Church of Christ, defined as those who keep God's commandments while living in a world that rejects those commandments. While salvation is only attained through faith in Jesus, the Adventists believe that once a person has been converted to their faith, his or her continuing conversion is manifested through adherence to a particular lifestyle. This includes abstaining from work or school on Saturdays, as well as not consuming alcohol, not smoking, and not eating certain foods such as pork and seafood. Adventists are enjoined to wear "sober" clothing and to exercise Christian restraint in their choices of entertainment. In practice, this means that they wear little or no jewelry. It also means that Antillean Adventists are not likely to be found in the Caribbean music dance clubs that provide one of the main outings for Antilleans in metropolitan France.

Inside the church all ethnic, national, and class divisions are to be erased. Because Adventists live "in the world," they are enjoined to be "model citizens," being obedient to the law and good workers. Their first loyalty, however, is ideally to the church and, through it, to God. In order to avoid conflicts in these loyalties, Adventists generally do not participate in trade unions or political movements. Despite the relatively large numbers of Adventists among the Antillean population in Paris, only once during my research did I encounter a church member in a meeting of an Antillean organization.

Separation from the world is facilitated by the organization of the church. Adventists can and often do commit a large amount of their time to working with the church, participating in Bible studies, choirs, and social organizations. The church is organized by its own members and, except for the pastor, positions of responsibility are filled through elections. These include members of committees, deacons, and elders, as well as the leaders of Sabbath school groups. While pastors have a certain moral authority in the church, the community itself decides how it will be organized and who will lead it. The congregation votes on the admission of new members and on all matters of discipline.

A very committed Adventist—and there are many—can spend several evenings each week either at the church or in missionary work. All Adventists are encouraged to give 10 percent of their income to the church and are often invited to make supplementary donations for other church activities. Members work to provide mutual assistance to one another, helping newcomers or visitors find housing or assisting the unemployed in finding work. The church demands that its members refrain from many types of behavior that are common among Antilleans in contemporary metropolitan France. In return, however, the Adventist church provides the "warm" atmosphere for which Antillean Catholic activists are so nostalgic.

Membership in the Seventh-Day Adventist Church seems to offer Antilleans refuge from the "coldness" of racism in French society. But the issues that confront Antilleans "in the world" can also appear in the church. While Antillean church members like Bernard are anxious to make Adventism central to who they are, putting aside any public assertion of Antillean identity, white church members I spoke with were quite willing to discuss the impact of an Antillean majority on the church in France. One white pastor told me that Antilleans were far more passionate in their style of worship than metropolitan French people, adding that he thought Antilleans were more "emotional" and less "cerebral" than French Adventists. Another pastor said that an Antillean majority made it necessary for the pastor to assume greater responsibilities. The Antilleans, he said, with their Catholic background, are less willing to take on leadership roles in the church. Such racist evaluations of Antillean congregants were not unusual, although they were in direct contradiction with Seventh-Day Adventist theology.

Conflicts over what one of the pastors called "church culture" led a group of white metropolitan French members and one pastor to form an all-white church in Paris in the late 1970s. Bernard told me that the French Adventist Federation disapproved of this initiative but that it had done nothing to interfere with the establishment of the separatist church. The pastor of the church told me that although Antilleans were dynamic members of any church, their passion discourages white members of the church, who are not used to such insistent activity. White church members feel dispossessed in churches "they helped to build before the arrival of many Antillean migrants." Echoing the arguments made by French officials about a "threshold of tolerance" in housing (a percentage of immigrants beyond which white French people would be driven out), the pastor told me that white church members began to feel displaced when Antillean membership grew beyond a third of any church's membership. When I asked if he thought Antilleans would leave if the white population in other churches grew beyond a third, he said he did not know. In any case, he said, that scenario is unlikely. Antillean and African immigrants are driving growth in the Seventh-Day Adventist Church all over Europe.

Bernard and other Antillean church members were disappointed that the Adventist federation had allowed the separatist church to be established. Ethnic differences were not supposed to be recognized in the church, they believed. But the members of the white church were old and had not recruited any new members in years. If they were doing God's will, their church would have grown. But racism in the church did raise hackles. One church member, a young schoolteacher from Martinique, found it odd that a person could be asked to leave the church for smoking or drinking—both relatively common infractions—but that practicing racial separatism was apparently not a sin serious enough for punishment.

The tension caused by the existence of one separatist white church was not enough to drive Antilleans from the Adventist church in Paris. For most members, the church provided a social structure and an identity that shielded Antilleans from most of the problems they would otherwise face in French society. The church provided them with a relatively homogeneous community, where being Antillean was secondary to other aspects of life. Adventists carry the church message to their family and friends, so that while they increase the church's membership, they also increase its Antillean character. In this way, the Adventist church begins to resemble a village in the islands.

RELIGIOUS IDENTITIES

At a mass organized by Antillean Catholics in France, I was given a handout with the words to several hymns in Creole. One of the verses read:

> Some have stiff hair, others have soft hair or even curly hair. Don't look to see who is black or white, Indian or *métis*, light skinned or mulatto. Together we must talk, together we must sing, together we must pray, together we must work, together we must search, together we must struggle.[4]

In a French Adventist publication, I found a Bible quote that reflected the same sentiment, this time in French: "There is neither Jew nor Greek, there is neither slave nor free, there is neither male nor female; for you are all one in Christ Jesus (Galatians 3:28)."[5] Antillean Catholics and Adventists provide two different approaches to the problem of Antillean identity in metropolitan France. These differences can be summed up in the contrasts between the two citations above. Both suggest that socially constructed differences are of little significance, that something unites people. Yet the contrasts in interpretation between the two groups were sharp.

The Catholic hymn, through its use of Creole and its focus on social divisions common in the Caribbean, is meant to help create a sense of community among Antillean parishioners while suggesting that these differences must not get in the way of community formation. The emphasis is on seeking common solutions to social problems and reinforcing a group identity as Antilleans. For Catholic activists, it is only through addressing these issues that Antilleans can become part of the universal Church in metropolitan France. The Church, in this view, must work to address worldly issues if it is to bring Antillean Catholics back. In fact, Antillean Catholic activists believe that the Church can remain universal only by reinforcing different cultural communities within the Church.

Adventists' ideas provide a sharp contrast to those of the Catholics. Creole is rarely heard in the Adventist churches in Paris, despite the fact that almost all of their membership is Antillean. But they believe that they must remain as open as possible to non–Creole-speaking converts. More important than the use of French in the Adventist Bible quote is the suggestion that ethnic differences no longer exist in the community of followers of Jesus. Worldly differences are supposed to be of little or no importance in the Adventist church; only the prophecies and commandments in the Bible should serve to organize the community. Only membership in the church matters.

Catholic Antillean activists link their efforts to address specifically Antillean issues to the social concerns of the Catholic Church. While the Church hierarchy limits these efforts with its own agenda, Antilleans can hope to integrate into metropolitan society as Catholics rather than as Antilleans, thus avoiding direct confrontation over the place of group identity in France. Instead, they become Catholics as Antilleans, which the Church accepts or even encourages. Adventists, on the other hand, strive to eliminate public identification as Antilleans. Ethnic identity among Adventists is a strictly private affair; in public they wish to be seen only as members of their church. The issue of ethnic group identity is avoided. Paradoxically, as Catholic Antilleans are integrated more fully into a majority French Church as Antillean Catholics, the Adventists, despite their best efforts, remain Antillean in the eyes of metropolitan French people.

Notes

1. *Le Nouvel Observateur,* February 22–28, 1996, 4–13.
2. *Le Point,* January 27, 1996, 50–59.
3. Alain Duhamel, "La spécificité protestante," *Le Point,* January 27, 1996.
4. "I tini chivé red, i tini chivé lis ou bien chivé bouklé, Pa gadé ki nègres, blan, zendien ou métis, chabinn ou milatres, Ansanm fô nou palé, ansanm fô nou chanté, ansamn fô nou priyé, Ansanm fô nou travay, ansanm fô nou chèché, ansamn fô nou lité." I have retained the Creole orthography used in the handout.
5. *Signes de vie,* 1st trimester 1989.

Further Reading

Brodwin, Paul. 2003. "Pentecostalism in Translation: Religion and the Production of Community in the Haitian Diaspora." *American Ethnologist* 30, no. 1: 85–101. This article shows how Pentecostalism, as practiced by Haitians in Guadeloupe, provides a cultural resource similar to that of Seventh-Day Adventism among Antilleans in France.

Carter, Donald Martin. 1997. *States of Grace: Senegalese in Italy and the New European Immigration.* Minneapolis: University of Minnesota Press. An analysis of how African immigrants in Turin build their religious identities across two continents in the context of changing Italian immigration policies and debates about national identity and religion in Italy and Africa.

Toulis, Nicole Rodriguez. 1997. *Believing Identity: Pentecostalism and the Mediation of Jamaican Ethnicity and Gender in England.* Oxford: Berg. An ethnography of religion, gender, and ethnicity among West Indians in Britain, this book provides insights into the way religion can be both a tool for integration and a refuge from racism.

Werbner, Pnina. 2002. *Imagined Diasporas Among Manchester Muslims: The Public Performance of Pakistani Transnational Identity Politics.* Santa Fe: School of American Research Press. An analysis of the role of religion in the formation of communities among South Asian Muslims in Britain, this book shows how religious ideas and practices are used and transformed through ethnic activism.

CHAPTER SEVEN

CONCLUSION: CREOLIZING FRANCE

CREOLE INTERNATIONAL

In late October 1989, I attended a celebration of International Creole Day in Evry, a suburb of Paris. Several of the associations I had been working with were involved in organizing the event, including Eloge and the Centre d'entraide et d'etude des antillais, guyanais, réunionnais (Center for Solidarity and Study of Antilleans, Guyanese, and Reunion Islanders, CEDAGR). According to the organizers, International Creole Day was created at a meeting in Louisiana of representatives from Creole-speaking countries in 1983. The representatives at that initial meeting came from Haiti, Guadeloupe, Martinique, Dominica, St. Lucia, French Guiana, Réunion, Mauritius, the Seychelles, and Louisiana. Although the Caribbean was heavily represented among them, organizers were quick to point out that the Creole-speaking countries also came from North America, Africa, and the Indian Ocean. From the beginning, the celebration was global.

International Creole Day was not marked in France until 1987 and is not a government-sponsored celebration. However, the organizers asserted that the growing number of Creole speakers there—predominantly Martinicans and Guadeloupans—made the Paris region a significant center for Creole languages. Organizers pointed out that distance from the islands did not mean that Creole speakers in France were not an important part of the linguistic community. They asserted that Creole was an essential part of the identity of

Antilleans in France. Celebrating International Creole Day would provide an opportunity to assert their attachment to the Antilles while also placing them in a broader international network of Creole-language activists.

Creole languages provided the focus of most of the day's activities, including workshops on the history of Creole languages and on reading and writing in Creole. There were tables of books in Creole and about Creole, cooking demonstrations, association representatives, storytelling, music, and other performances. The day began with a few speeches welcoming attendees—a few hundred people—in several different Creoles. Speaking in French, a representative of the CEDAGR defined some of the day's objectives. While Creole languages would serve as the key to the proceedings, he said, organizers intended to go beyond language. The event would create a context in which *créolité* (Creoleness) could be seen as a legitimate form of identity. We will demonstrate, here in France, our deep attachment to our *patrimoine* (cultural wealth), he said. Speaking Creole is a fundamental part of who we are, but it is tied to other aspects of our identities, including food, music, and dance. Our goal is to put an end to the subordination of Creole languages to other languages, including French, and to show that it can be used in all contexts. We also need to end the "official ignorance" of Creole on the part of government authorities. Equal recognition of our language, he concluded, is part of our work to achieve equal recognition for our *cultures*.

By putting *culture* in the plural, he called attention to one of the unusual features of the day's events. Although most of the participants were Antillean, the "international" label referred to linkages between societies that shared similar but not identical languages. There was not one Creole, but many. I attended a workshop on reading and writing in Creole. The organizers, including two members of the CEDAGR, drew on a writing system developed by a group of Antillean linguists, organized as the Groupe de recherches et d'études en espace créole (Research Group on Creole Spaces, GEREC).[1] The GEREC system was designed to emphasize the differences between Creole languages and French and at the same time create a kind of written uniformity between Creoles.

This approach to reading and writing gave Creole languages an unusual political potential. They were, as the day's opening speaker had noted, a part of the identity and cultural wealth of Antilleans and of other groups. This meant that they were a marker of ethnic identity in France. For nationalists in the Antilles and elsewhere, they also represented national languages. However, with their decision to recognize their links to other Creole languages, the organizers of International Creole Day created an identity that transcended international borders. This was one of the core ideas of *créolité*. To be Creole was to identify with a history and a cultural heritage, but it was also a new kind of identity that transcended the narrow confines of nations.

Their position was a direct challenge to dominant French thinking about nations and cultures. Being Creole transcended borders while preserving the particularities of its constituent groups; French thinking emphasized a world of discrete cultures. A person could not be both French and something else at the same time. This had been translated into policies that had long worked to eliminate regional languages—including Creole—in France. I was surprised, then, to learn that in 2000, Jack Lang, the minister of education, had decided to create a prestigious new teaching degree in Creole. Announcing that the first exams leading to the degree would take place in 2002, Lang said that it was important for schools to support regional identities in France. "Our education goals are the same throughout France," he said, "but unity does not require uniformity."[2]

FRENCH CULTURE, BLACK SKINS

This was a surprising statement for a French government minister to make, especially the minister of education. The national education system was created with the objective of establishing uniformity in France, turning diverse peoples—a diversity marked, among other things, by language—into French citizens. Linguistic uniformity was written into the French constitution, and in 1999 President Chirac rejected the idea of amending the constitution to allow France to ratify the European Charter for Regional or Minority Languages. This seemed more in line with the direction taken by French policymakers during the 1980s and 1990s. Faced with increasing pressure to recognize the ethnic diversity of immigrant groups in France, political leaders and intellectuals insisted on a return to the fundamental values of the French republic. Elements of diversity, including language, but also religion and ethnicity, were supposed to become private, leaving only individual citizens of the republic visible in the public sphere.

France has long been a country of immigration; the 1990s were not the first time that growing diversity led to national debates about French identity. But the immigrants who arrived in France after World War II were qualitatively different from those in the past. French policymakers and intellectuals have described these immigrants—primarily dark-skinned people from the third world—as especially difficult to assimilate. They brought, it is often claimed, differences that made them more difficult to integrate into French society than previous immigrants. The ongoing debate about "Islamic scarves" in public schools is emblematic of this perspective on immigrants. The meaning of *culture* in France and the definition of how people may participate in it are both central to these debates.

In theory, anyone may become French. The ideals of "republican universalism" define the nation as a community of individuals, not a collection of cultures. Individual citizens may choose to become part of that community. When they do so, they also choose to adhere to a set of values that includes putting aside ethnic or religious affiliations in public life. Since the end of the nineteenth century, French governments have developed ideologies and institutions—especially schools—that are meant to ensure that everyone in France understands and adheres to those common values. The fear that religious or ethnic groups in France might form and act as "communities" in the public sphere is central to policy debates on immigration. The culture of the French nation remains predominantly individualist.

But republican universalism has long competed with a more closed version of French national identity. In this view, being French requires roots in the history and territory of the nation, in "the land and the dead" (Maurice Barrès, quoted in Todorov 1989, 257). This approach draws on the idea that France is historically Catholic and rural; urban society is rejected for being too cosmopolitan and too open to diversity. These views have long been associated with the extreme right, but they have occasionally been promoted by the left. This has been most evident in efforts to emphasize the importance of regional cultures and folklore as having contributed to an idea of a greater, "true" French *culture*. Closed nationalism rejects the possibility that immigrants can become French, asserting that they will always remain tied to their cultures of origin.

Race remains largely absent from these definitions of French identity. French identity is formed around notions of shared culture, territory, and language, all organized by the state, which is understood to be an expression of the sovereign people. This understanding of identity is extended to an ordering of the world in which everyone is assigned to one culture, which is associated with one state and one territory. Immigrants, in this view, carry their culture with them to France and, unless they can find a way to completely adopt French culture, they will always be part of their culture of origin. This logic leads to interesting consequences for the children of immigrants, who are simply called "second-generation immigrants," although, of course, they have not immigrated anywhere. Here culture takes on the character of a substance that is passed on through descent. This form of cultural transmission is imperfect, however, leaving the children of immigrants "between two cultures," suffering from a form of anomie that makes them particularly susceptible to the dangerous influences of their cultures of origin.

Culture becomes, then, a convenient gloss for something that "looks" like race (cf. Balibar 1991; Hargreaves 1995; Stolcke 1995). In America, when people speak of "race," they generally mean black people, not some abstract concept. Similarly, when the notion of *immigrés* (immigrants) is invoked in France, the topic of conversation generally veers toward North Africans, with possible detours concerning Muslims in general. In a world of discrete cultures, certain cultures are thought to make their members especially resistant to adaptation to French society. Although the French frequently use the term "immigrant" as a euphemism for a particular group, such discussions focus on cultural difference. Discrimination and exclusion of putative foreigners from France is considered to be primarily a matter of culture, but of cultures that constrain people in ways that resemble race.

Even without the notion of race, however, there is racism in France. Rather than being based on beliefs about a putative biological hierarchy among humans, racism in France refers to an unjust invocation of cultural differences. From this perspective, when municipal officials justify the exclusion of immigrants from public housing by invoking a "threshold of tolerance" of cultural diversity beyond which French people will be driven out, they are engaging in racist behavior. Similarly, suggesting that Antillean culture drives them to have loud parties in their apartments can be seen as a form of racism because it looks to cultural difference to explain behavior that might better be explained in other ways.

This kind of racism was especially evident during the 1990s, as concerns about poverty and crime were increasingly ethnicized in France. Failing schools, poorly maintained public housing, and street crime came to be associated with the working-class suburbs where many immigrants and their descendants live. Social disorder (*insecurité*) and social exclusion became major themes in politics. Immigrants and their neighborhoods were often the implicit—and sometimes explicit, especially in the case of the *sans papiers*, or illegal immigrants—object of these debates. The failure to make recent immigrants and their children into upstanding French citizens was blamed on the immigrants' cultures of origin, rather than on any failings of French public policy. France in the 1990s seemed to be coming apart at the seams.

Despite hopeful signs of integration, such as the victory of France's multicultural World Cup soccer team in 1998, immigrants seemed forced to pay an impossibly high price to become French. Even if they were willing to give up public attachment to their cultures of origin, it was not clear that French people were willing to acknowledge their integration in return. For every positive sign of inclusion, there was an equal and opposite sign of rejection. After the 1998 World Cup came the 2002 success of far right anti-immigrant leader Jean-Marie Le Pen in the first round of presidential elections, suggesting, if only for a few weeks, that a substantial portion of the French electorate held extreme views.

ASSIMILATION AND ITS DISCONTENTS

The growth of racism and the increasingly strident assertions of republican fundamentalism by French leaders have had a sharp impact on Antilleans in the Caribbean and France. Antilleans were long willing to pay the cultural price required to be accepted into French society. There is a stereotype of Antilleans who aspire to upward mobility, working hard in school and learning to speak elegant French. They are said to be "more French than the French" and are always eager to prove their understanding of the essential elements of French culture. Few accounts of the initial "Islamic scarf" affair in 1989 noted that one such Martinican was the catalyst for the affair itself. Ernest Chenière was the principal who decided to expel the girls for wearing their scarves in class. He came to metropolitan France from Martinique with his family in the mid-1950s. Following a classic French educational trajectory, Chenière became a schoolteacher, something he apparently regarded as more of a mission than a career. As a teacher and a principal, Chenière symbolized the values of the French Republic, where education was seen as the key to making the French nation. Those were the values he was defending when he expelled the scarf-wearing girls. But as a Martinican, he was himself a symbol of the growing minorities who were threatening to reshape French society. This contradiction has been at the center of Antillean difficulties in France.

For many Antilleans, the ideals of freedom and equality have long been associated with the French Republic. The Republic exported those ideas to Caribbean slave societies during the revolution of 1789 and finally made good on the promise of freedom in 1848. Assimilation into the Republic as equal citizens was seen by many Antilleans as a key to overcoming the political and economic domination of the *békés*. Consequently anticolonial ideology in Martinique and Guadeloupe emphasized greater inclusion into France rather than independence. The pursuit of these ideals resulted, after World War II, in the political transformation of Martinique and Guadeloupe into French overseas departments.

Departmentalization played an essential role in helping overcome the political power of the *békés*, but in other ways the promise of assimilation has not been fulfilled. The standard of living in the Antilles has never reached that in France. The process of political and economic incorporation into France has led to the destruction of the local economy in Guadeloupe and Martinique. Local production has been replaced by French imports, making the Antilles modern consumer societies, at least for those who have jobs and can afford expensive consumer goods. But there are sharp inequalities in the Antilles and a disproportionate part of the population—when compared with France—is dependent on assistance from the French welfare state. This transformation has played an important role in Antillean emigration to France.

Despite education in French schools and assimilation into French society as full citizens, Antilleans have never been recognized as truly French by most French people. Martinique and Guadeloupe are rarely recognized as part of France when most French people describe their country. Martinicans and Guadeloupans are still seen as representatives of the exotic, sensual tropics, fundamentally different from people in metropolitan France. Because the Antilles chose assimilation in an era when most other colonies were seeking independence, French social scientists and intellectuals have long wondered if there was something wrong with the Antilles. Such questions are unlikely to be raised about Alsace, the Basque region, or Brittany, which might have legitimate reasons to seek independence but are not really expected to because deep down "everyone" knows they are French. Despite their long attachment to France, the opposite assumption is made about the Antilles.

Pushed by failing economies and pulled by expectations of upward mobility, as well as by government recruiters, Antilleans have moved to France in large numbers since the early 1960s. The Antillean population in France rivals the populations of Martinique and Guadeloupe, constituting a "third island," mostly dispersed around the Paris region. Antilleans were brought to France to work in civil service jobs, as health care workers, customs officers, and subway and postal workers. These were jobs noncitizens could not hold; and secure jobs that permitted the first generation of migrants to attain a standard of living not available to "real" foreign workers. Economic crises and government cutbacks since the 1970s have significantly reduced recruitment for those sorts of jobs, so there has been less formal effort to recruit Antilleans to come to France. Those who do come—along with the children of those who are already there—face a very different job market, where citizenship plays a less significant role and discrimination based on a perception of foreign origins can be decisive.

Their experience of life in metropolitan France has led many Antilleans to question their own Frenchness. They are deeply knowledgeable about French ways of doing and thinking about things. By right and by law they are French and should benefit from that status. But outside of public employment, they are subject to the same kinds of discrimination in jobs and housing experienced by other immigrants. Faced with a rising tide of racism and a growing sense of not being quite French, Antilleans formed many associations in the 1980s in France, just as other immigrant groups did. Speaking through those organizations, Antilleans in France have began to demand recognition as a distinct community in France.

Faced with the contradictions and failures of assimilation, Antilleans have long experimented with alternate ideologies with which they can build their claims for recognition. Among these, the development of *créolité* has proven especially popular among Antillean activists in France. For Martinicans and Guadeloupans in France, *créolité* legitimizes their cultural difference but also asserts that their difference is different from other differences. Others—immigrants from North Africa, for instance—represent something totally different from French society. But Antilleans are at the same time both cultural insiders and outsiders. *Créolité* calls attention to the links between Antillean *culture* and France. As Creoles, however, Antilleans may be the wave of the future. *Créolité* is also popular because it provides Antilleans with the capacity to claim that their identity transcends France.

CARIBBEAN IDENTITY RECLAIMED

In France, *culture* is the main battleground for forging identity. This can take many forms, from efforts to form a common national culture through the schools to substantial subsidies given to arts organizations to create representations of high French art. The form and content of choices made by Antillean activists in France draw on many of the same tools used by the French government to construct their own alternatives. Each of the groups I have examined focuses on a different aspect of identity construction and each has a particular way of constructing and legitimizing a sense of Antillean cultural community in metropolitan France. What they all have in common is an overarching interest in cultural identity, in the sense of a set of characteristics that can be represented through art or described by social science. Each of these groups of activists seeks to represent Antillean *culture* as a recognizable alternative to dominant notions of French identity. In this way, they hope to convince other Antilleans of the need for a legitimate Antillean identity and, at the same time, convince French policymakers that they should recognize Antillean distinctiveness on their terms.

One of the key tools used by the French government in creating the idea of a national culture is the idea of a *patrimoine culturel*, or cultural wealth, that is shared by all French people. This notion includes the cultures of French regions, seen as elements of folklore that have contributed to the greater French whole. Having found themselves defined as cultural outsiders, Antilleans in France have also turned to the idea of a *patrimoine culturel* as a tool to represent their identity in France and build community among Antilleans there. This was the tactic used by the Eloge theater troupe. In their performances, they drew on nostalgia for a lost Antillean world. Faced with experiences of racism and rejection in France, they turned their back on assimilation and chose instead to create a distinct social world for themselves that they connected, through their performances, with the Antilles rather than Paris. Antillean audiences welcomed the escape from life in France that these performances offered, coupled, as they often were, with an evening spent among other Antilleans. However, neither the theater troupe members nor their audiences had much hope of returning to the Antilles. The Eloge performances did not provide much in the way of critical tools for making sense of Antillean experiences in France.

Stand-Fast members were also eager to assert an idea of Antillean *patrimoine* in France, but they chose to claim a distinct place within French society. The differences between Stand-Fast and Eloge were partially rooted in their different experiences of migration. While Eloge members were primarily first-generation migrants raised in the Antilles, the members of Stand-Fast were mostly born in France of immigrant parents. They had few personal experiences of life in the Antilles. Instead of nostalgia, they drew on forms of high art—classical music, dance, fashion, painting—to create what they viewed as a particular Caribbean aesthetic. Their objective was to transform French high art itself, in effect *creolizing* French culture. Although this approach was meant to address the experiences of Antilleans in France, it was never clear if Stand-Fast would be able to transcend the nostalgia of older Antilleans for life in the Antilles or the appeal of pop culture to younger generations born in metropolitan France.

Since the 1980s, political officials in France have become increasingly strident in their assertions of republican fundamentalism. Yet they have also quietly shifted a great deal of the responsibility for administering the programs of the French welfare state to nonprofit associations. By providing assistance to nonprofits organized and run by immigrants, policymakers have tacitly recognized the idea that immigrants may have needs that arise out of their distinct experiences in France. The social scientists, social workers, journalists, government bureaucrats, and students who joined together to form the CEDAGR were part of this movement, working to create recognition for *le culturel* in a field, the French welfare state, where *le social*, or social class, had long been the only legitimate form of social division. Their approach ran the risk of making Antilleans in France appear to be a group always in need of assistance, something they feared had already happened in the Antilles. In the 1990s, as policy debates about immigration began to be subsumed in debates about social exclusion, the CEDAGR approach began to look increasingly inadequate. The ethnicization of poverty debates probably worked in favor of groups like the CEDAGR, but the territorialization of those debates in the working-class suburbs could just as easily return the focus of policymakers to social class, reasserting the primacy of *le social* over *le culturel*.

Antillean religious activists seem at first to provide a counterexample to the strategies I just described. Rather than assert Antillean cultural identity as defining the place of Antilleans within metropolitan French society, these activists place Antilleans in the sphere of religion, thus removing them from debates about national identity. Catholic activists, however, link this strategy to an attempt to restore the central role the Catholic Church played in the Antilles. Lay activists seek to creolize the Catholic Church in France, providing an anchor for the Antillean community while at the same time participating in the more universal objectives of Catholicism. They work to move the Church toward providing both a physical and an ideological space in which Antillean cultural identity can be reinforced; they also see Catholicism as a tool that they can use to transcend the rejection they experience in France.

Seventh-Day Adventists provide an ideology in which Antillean origin or identity ceases to have significance. In some ways, this group poses the most radical challenge to the French state, since it rejects the existence of a cultural inside or outside, arguing that Adventism represents a universal identity that goes beyond concerns with national identity. Even in its denial of the significance of cultural identity, Adventist identity goes some way to providing Antilleans with the perception that they are integrating into French society. At the very least, the exotic forms of behavior that metropolitan French people associate with Antilleans are absent from the lives of Adventists. Because the church is relatively homogeneous, the Antillean aspects of its membership can remain mostly unquestioned and private. Furthermore, Adventists are enjoined to continue to carry out the church's mission among their friends and families. In this manner, even while proclaiming an intention to bring their message to all people in France, the members can maintain the church's Antillean character. Although many members suggest that they feel a stronger sense of community with Adventists of any origin than with non-Adventist Antilleans (a perspective apparently not shared by the dissident white members of the church), they continue to meet in their church almost entirely with other Antilleans.

Faced with broken promises of assimilation and a rising tide of racism, Antillean activists have developed a wide range of strategies to create and assert ideas about what it means to be Antillean in France. Because they draw on some of the central terms and concepts that make French identity, it is tempting to conclude that the form and content of their activities is largely determined by dominant French discourses. But this is only a partial explanation. Given their historic ties, it is difficult to determine where to draw the line between Antillean and French cultures. The groups I have examined in this volume built ties across the Atlantic that also inspire their actions. They provide more than a mirror image of the formation of identities in France. They also point to ways in which their actions may succeed in changing—in creolizing—French society itself.

CREOLIZED FRANCE

When I first began my research in the late 1980s, it was difficult to imagine that ethnic activists would succeed in changing dominant ideas about French identity. French leaders were willing to acknowledge the existence of racism and work on policies to prevent it. But they were also anxious to reassert the fundamental ideas that had contributed to the formation of the French Republic. These included a secular state—one in which scarf-wearing girls in public schools had no place—and a population of individual citizens whose ethnic, regional, or religious identifications were private, of no concern to public policy. If ethnic social service associations like the CEDAGR were allowed to acquire legitimacy, it was only because they provided services that contributed to making Antilleans complete French citizens. There was no question of creating a place in French public life for ethnic communities. Above all, France was not going to become multicultural. In the late 1980s and early 1990s, French political leaders and intellectuals uttered that word with evident disdain, as if it were a disease they could catch from too much intellectual intercourse with Americans.

Yet the self-assured representation of French national identity demonstrated in the bicentennial of the revolution parade faded into memory, it was replaced with other representations that seemed to hint at a willingness to accept some kind of difference in the public sphere. The wild celebrations of the French victory in the 1998 Soccer World Cup promoted the idea that France was now willing to accept that it had become diverse, perhaps even multicultural. Comparisons with the much less diverse teams fielded by other European countries suggested to many French commentators that perhaps diversity led to strength. The commemoration of the 1848 abolition of slavery also seemed to suggest that the place of diversity in France was being rethought. While Antilleans were understandably suspicious of French intentions, events were probably organized to impress other immigrants and French citizens with the values that, the government seemed to be saying, had been born out of 1848. Finally, in 2000, the minister of education asserted that national unity did not require uniformity. Did this mean that dominant models of French identity had been transformed?

I had initially expected that Antilleans, with their historic ties to French society, would create identities that mirrored the main ideas that made up French national identity. To a certain extent they did, by drawing on French notions of culture and society with which to formulate their demands. Inspired by the ideas proposed by the authors of the *Eloge de la créolité*, however, they also worked to transcend some of those French concepts. Stand-Fast, for instance, refused to situate its activism in the realm of folk culture, which would certainly have offered a niche compatible with the ideas promoted by the French government. Instead, they worked to situate their ethnic art as a part of high culture. They planned to draw in artists, musicians, and designers from the rest of the Caribbean as well, pointing to the ways their identity transcended the narrow limits of nationalism. This sort of global perspective was clearly at work in the International Creole Day as well. Antilleans in France are not merely creating an alternative identity to French national models. They are proposing to rethink the limits of cultural identity altogether.

French policymakers are being pressured to rethink the forms of French identity, aside from the work of Antillean activists. The European Union provides a different context in which the French idea of the nation-state is being pushed to change. But the push from within, from immigrant activists like those we have examined in this volume, is toward a new kind of model of society. It is a push toward creolization. France is being creolized.

Notes

1. The GEREC has been renamed the GEREC-F: Groupe de recherches et d'études en espace créole et francophone.
2. Cited in *Le Monde*, October 20, 2000.

Further Reading

Schiller, Nina Glick, and Georges Fouron. 2001. *Georges Woke Up Laughing: Long-Distance Nationalism and the Search for Home.* Durham, N.C.: Duke University Press. This ethnographic study of Haitian migration to the United States examines how categories like nation, ethnicity, race, and gender have been reconfigured as immigrants and their children think of themselves across national boundaries.

Vergès, Françoise. 1999. *Monsters and Revolutionaries: Colonial Family Romance and Métissage.* Durham, N.C.: Duke University Press. Focusing on Réunion, a French overseas department in the Indian Ocean, this book examines the interplay of French republican ideologies, racism, and colonialism in creating hybrid forms of identity.

Werbner, Pnina, and Tariq Modood, eds. 1997. *Debating Cultural Hybridity: Multi-Cultural Identities and the Politics of Anti-Racism.* London: Zed. A collection of essays exploring the meaning of cultural hybridity in social theory and in practice with a particular emphasis on assertions of hybridity in Europe.

Glossary

Action Catholique—a movement founded by the Catholic Church in the 1920s to create organizations, including youth groups and workers associations, designed to bring a Catholic perspective to secular debates in France.

Agence nationale pour l'insertion et la promotion des travailleurs d'outre-mer (ANT)—National Agency for the Promotion and Insertion of Workers from Overseas, a French government agency that facilitates migration to and from the overseas departments and territories, replaced the BUMIDOM in 1982.

Antillanité—usually associated with the work of Edouard Glissant, the ideology of "Caribbean-ness" calls for Antillean identities to be grounded in the Caribbean, rather than in Europe or Africa.

Antilles—broadly, the islands of the Caribbean. In France, the term is usually used to refer to Martinique, Guadeloupe, and French Guiana.

Arrondissement—an urban administrative district. Paris is divided into twenty arrondissements.

Aumônerie Catholique Antilles-Guyane de Paris—the Antillean and Guyanese Catholic Center of Paris.

Bastille Day—celebrated on July 14, Bastille Day is a national holiday that commemorates the storming of the Bastille prison by the people of Paris in 1789, often considered the starting event of the French Revolution.

Beauharnais, Joséphine de—(1763–1814), born Joséphine Marie-Josèphe Rose Tascher de La Pagerie, daughter of a Martinican planter and slave owner, married Napoleon Bonaparte in 1796.

Béké—local whites in Martinique and Guadeloupe.

Bélè—a popular form of drumming music in Martinique.

Beur—Arab in *verlan*, a kind of slang that more or less inverts the letters of words to form new words, associated with youth, immigrant, and working-class subcultures of French suburbs.

Bonaparte, Napoléon—(1769–1821), born in Corsica, became a French general and emperor of France between 1804 and 1815, known for his military innovation and for reinstating slavery in the French colonies in 1802.

Bonapartist—in nineteenth- and early-twentieth-century France, an ideology that asserted the need for a strong, possibly dictatorial leader for French society, rather than a republic.

Boudin—blood sausage, common in both French and Antillean cuisines. The Antillean version is substantially spicier than the *boudin* usually found in metropolitan France.

Bureau pour les migrations intéressant les départements d'outre-mer (BUMIDOM)—created in 1963, a French government agency that facilitated the migration of Antilleans to metropolitan France. Replaced in 1982 by the ANT.

Calalou de crabe—a thin gumbo made with herbs and crabmeat, often served in the French Antilles.

Centrale syndicale des travailleurs martiniquais (CSTM)—Union of Martinican Workers, one of the main organizations pursuing independence from France for Martinique.

Centre d'entraide et d'etude des antillais, guyanais, réunionnais (CEDAGR)—Center for Solidarity and Study of Antilleans, Guyanese, and Réunion Islanders.

Colombo de porc—a pork curry, common in Antillean cuisine.

Confédération française de travailleurs chrétiens (CFTC)—French Confederation of Christian Workers, a French trade union with ties to the Catholic Church.

Conseil Général—General Council, an elected body that governs a *département* (department) in France. Martinique and Guadeloupe are each one department.

Conseil Régional—Regional Council, an elected body that governs a *région* (region) in France. Although a region usually covers several departments, Martinique and Guadeloupe each form one region.

Coulis—term used in Martinique and Guadeloupe to refer to people of East Indian descent.

Créole—refers to the vernacular language of Guadeloupe, Martinique, and a variety of other Caribbean islands and other countries, as well as to people born in those places.

Créolité—an ideology that asserts the originality of Antillean cultures, pointing to their capacity to continually reinvent themselves while drawing on their European, African, and Asian heritages. Usually attributed to a manifesto written by three Martinican intellectuals (Bernabé et al. 1989).

Culture—culture, commonly used in France to describe the distinct way of life of a people, most often linked to a territory and usually invoked as a reified thing that groups possess.

Culturel, le—ethnic or traditional aspects of life, usually associated with regional or immigrant minorities in France and contrasted with *le social*.

Damier—Martinican dance, accompanied by singing, that simulates combat between two usually male dancers.

Département—a French territorial unit, governed by a *préfet*, who represents the central government, and a *conseil general*, a local elected body. France is divided into one hundred *départements*.

Départements d'outre-mer (DOM)—overseas departments, including Martinique and Guadeloupe.

Doudouiste—used by Antillean activists and cultural critics to describe literature, music, art, or ideology that presents the Antilles or Antilleans as a kind of exotic, tropical fantasy.

Entre deux cultures—between two cultures.

Exclusif—trade policy that required French colonies to export their goods exclusively to France and to import goods only from France.

Fonds d'action et de soutien pour l'intégration et la lutte contre les discriminations (FASILD)—Action Fund for the Promotion of Integration and the Struggle Against Discrimination, French government agency charged with integration policy, formerly known as the FAS.

Fonds d'action sociale pour les travailleurs immigrés et leurs familles(FAS)—Social Action Fund for Immigrant Workers and their Families, French government agency charged with integration policy, now the FASILD.

Foulard islamiques—head scarves worn by Muslim women and girls in France, the source of great controversy.

Front National—National Front, the largest extreme right party in France, associated with its leader, Jean-Marie Le Pen, and with strident anti-immigrant rhetoric.

Gadézafé—an Antillean fortune-teller or healer.

Galère, la—the struggle; usually the distressed conditions and meager opportunities faced by working-class and immigrant youth in the suburbs of French cities.

Gens de couleur libre—free black and mixed-race Antilleans who, prior to the end of slavery, formed an educated and activist middle class and after the end of slavery played a central role in efforts to assimilate the Antilles into France.

Grands blancs—wealthy plantation-owning whites in the French Antilles.

Groupe de recherches et d'études en espace créole (GEREC)—Research Group on Creole Space, a group of intellectuals, primarily but not exclusively Antillean, who work to promote Creole language and culture.

Gwoka—Guadeloupan traditional drumming music.

Immigrés—immigrants.

Indépendantiste—a person who favors independence for Martinique and Guadeloupe.

Insecurité—social disorder; usually emphasizing crime rates in French cities.

Jeunesses ouvrières chrétiennes (JOC)—Young Christian Workers, a Catholic movement to organize working-class youth, part of Action Catholique.

Kanaks—the indigenous people of New Caledonia.

Laicité—secularism; in France, an ideology which asserts that the state should remain neutral in religious affairs and religious expression should be excluded from public life.

Marabout—an African fortune-teller or healer.

Marrons—escaped slaves who formed their own communities in the plantation societies of the Americas, also used as a metaphor to describe anyone who resists French domination in the Antilles.

Métèque quelconque—slang for average immigrant or foreigner.

Métis—a person of mixed heritage, either cultural or racial.

Métissage—the process of cultural or racial mixing.

Métropole—mainland France, as opposed to the colonies or overseas departments and territories.

Métropolitain—a person from mainland France.

Musée National des Arts et Traditions Populaires (ATP)—National Museum for Popular Traditions and Arts, France's main museum of folklore.

Nèg congo—a Créole term referring to Africans who arrived in the Antilles after the end of slavery.

Négritude—ideology that emphasizes the links between people of African descent, often associated with the writings of Aimé Césaire, Léon Gontron Damas, and Léopold Senghor.

Noir—black, used in the Antilles to refer to descendants of African slaves and in France, to skin color.

Patrimoine culturel—cultural wealth, used in France to refer to both material things such as monuments, art, and architecture, as well as ideas and practices.

Petits blancs—poor and working-class whites in the Antilles, as distinguished from *grands blancs*.

Piment—scotch bonnet or habanero pepper, commonly used as a condiment in the Antilles.

Pré-délinquance, en—used to describe "at-risk" youth.

Préfet—local representative of the central Paris government, usually charged with administration of a department.

Région—a French territorial unit governed by an elected *conseil regional*, usually made up of a number of *départements*. Martinique and Guadeloupe each form one region; there are twenty-two French *régions*.

Rhum—rum.

Sans papiers—undocumented people in France, often illegal immigrants and refugees.

Savane, la—the central square and park in Fort-de-France, Martinique.

Service municipal d'action culturelle (SERMAC)—Municipal Service for Cultural Action, the SERMAC is an agency of the city of Fort-de-France that organizes and promotes the arts.

Shrub—a drink made from rum, in which orange peels and other fruit have soaked.

Social, le—term used in France to describe areas in which government policies are required to reduce the structural tensions brought on by class differences.

Société des Amis des Noirs—Society of Friends of the Blacks, an eighteenth-century antislavery organization.

SOS Racisme—one of the best known French antiracism organizations, founded in 1984.

Syro-Libanais—Antilleans of Middle Eastern background.

Tchimbé rèd—a common Creole salutation, literally "stand firm."

Ti'punch—a popular drink in the Antilles and among Antilleans in France, usually a mixture of rum, lime, and sugar.

Travailleurs étrangers—foreign workers.

Voyant—fortune-teller.

Z'oreilles—metropolitan French person in the Antilles.

Zouk—popular dance music in the French Antilles.

References

Abu-Lughod, Lila. 1991. "Writing Against Culture." In Richard G. Fox, ed., *Recapturing Anthropology: Working in the Present*, 137–162. Santa Fe: School of American Research Press.

Affergan, F. 1983. *Anthropologie à la Martinique*. Paris: Presses de la Fondation Nationale des Sciences Politiques.

Agence nationale pour l'insertion et la promotion des travailleurs d'outre-mer. 1985. *Annuaire des associations d'originaires d'outre-mer*. Paris: ANT.

_____. 1988. *Annuaire des associations d'originaires d'outre-mer*. Paris: ANT.

Alexander, Jack. 1977. "The Culture of Race in Middle-Class Kingston, Jamaica." *American Ethnologist* 4, no. 3: 413–435.

André, Jacques. 1983. "L'identité ou le retour du même." *Temps modernes* 441–442: 2026–2037.

Appadurai, Arjun. 1991. "Global Ethnoscapes: Notes and Queries for a Transnational Anthropology." In Richard G. Fox, ed., *Recapturing Anthropology: Working in the Present*, 191–210. Santa Fe: School of American Research Press.

Balibar, Etienne. 1991. "Is There a 'Neo-Racism'?" In Etienne Balibar and Immanuel Wallerstein, eds., *Race, Nation, Class: Ambiguous Identities*. New York: Verso.

Bancel, Nicolas, Pascal Blanchard, and Françoise Vergès. 2003. *La république coloniale: Essai sur une utopie*. Paris: Albin Michel.

Bangou, Henri. 1989. *La révolution et l'esclavage à la Guadeloupe: 1789–1802*. Paris: Editions Sociales.

Bastien, Daniel. 1989a. Editorial: Au-delà des turquoises. *Autrement Série Monde*. 41:9–11.

Bastien, Daniel. 1989b. Le casse-tête économique. *Autrement Série Monde*. 41:77–85.

Baumann, Gerd. 1996. *Contesting Culture: Discourses of Identity in Multi-Ethnic London.* Cambridge: Cambridge University Press.

Bébel-Gisler, Dany. 1976. *La langue créole, force jugulée: Etude socio-linguistique des rapports de force entre le créole et le français aux Antilles.* Paris: L'Harmattan.

Beriss, David. 1990. "Scarves, Schools, and Segregation: The Foulard Affair." *French Politics and Society* 8: 1–13.

Bernabé, Jean, Patrick Chamoiseau, and Raphaël Confiant. 1989. *Eloge de la créolité.* Paris: Gallimard.

———. 1993. *Eloge de la créolité: In Praise of Creoleness.* Translated by M. B. Taleb-Khyar. Paris: Gallimard.

Bertho, Catherine. 1980. "L'invention de la Bretagne: Genèse sociale d'un stéréotype." *Actes de la recherche en sciences sociales* 35: 45–61.

Birnbaum, Pierre. 1993. *"La France aux Français": Histoire des haines nationalistes.* Paris: Seuil.

———. 2001. *The Idea of France.* Translated by M. B. DeBevoise. New York: Hill & Wang.

Blatt, David. 1997. "Immigrant Politics in a Republican Nation." In Alec G. Hargreaves and Mark McKinney, eds., *Post-Colonial Cultures in France,* 40–55. London: Routledge.

Blérald, Alain-Philippe. 1981. *Négritude et politique aux Antilles.* Paris: Editions Caribéennes.

———. 1988. *La question nationale en Guadeloupe et en Martinique.* Paris: L'Harmattan.

Boëldieu, Julien, and Catherine Borrel. 2000. "La proportion d'immigrés est stable depuis 25 ans." *INSEE première* 748.

Bongie, Chris. 2001. "A Street Named Bissette: Nostalgia, Memory, and the Cent-Cinquantenaire of the Abolition of Slavery in Martinique (1848–1998)." *South Atlantic Quarterly* 100, no. 1: 215–257.

Bourdieu, Pierre. 1979. *La distinction: Critique sociale du jugement.* Paris: Minuit.

———. 1981. "La représentation politique." *Actes de la recherche en sciences sociales.* 36–37: 3–24.

Breton, André. 1972. *Martinique: Charmeuse de serpents.* Paris: Jean-Jacques Pauvert.

Brodwin, Paul. 2003a. "Marginality and Subjectivity in the Haitian Diaspora." *Anthropological Quarterly* 76, no. 3: 383–410.

———. 2003b. "Pentecostalism in Translation: Religion and the Production of Community in the Haitian Diaspora." *American Ethnologist* 30, no. 1: 85–101.

Brown, Jacqueline Nassy. 1998. "Black Liverpool, Black America, and the Gendering of Diasporic Space." *Cultural Anthropology* 13, no. 3: 291–325.

Browne, Katherine. 2002. "Creole Economics and the *Débrouillard*: From Slave-Based Adaptations to the Informal Economy in Martinique." *Ethnohistory* 49, no. 2: 373–403.

Brubaker, Rogers. 1992. *Citizenship and Nationhood in France and Germany.* Cambridge: Harvard University Press.

Burton, Richard D. E. 1994. *La famille coloniale: La Martinique et la mère patrie, 1789–1992*. Paris: L'Harmattan.

Burton, Richard D. E., and Fred Réno, eds. 1995. *French and West Indian: Martinique, Guadeloupe, and French Guiana Today*. Charlottesville: University Press of Virginia.

Carter, Donald Martin. 1997. *States of Grace: Senegalese in Italy and the New European migration*. Minneapolis: University of Minnesota Press.

Césaire, Aimé. 1983. *Cahier d'un retour au pays natal*. Paris: Présence Africaine.

———. 2001. *Notebook of a Return to the Native Land*. Translated and edited by Clayton Eshleman and Annette Smith. Middletown, Conn.: Wesleyan University Press.

Chamoiseau, Patrick. 1986. *Chronique des sept misères*. Paris: Gallimard.

———. 1992. *Texaco*. Paris: Gallimard.

———. 1997. *Ecrire en pays dominé*. Paris: Gallimard.

Chevalier, Louis. 1973. *Laboring Classes and Dangerous Classes in Paris During the First Half of the Nineteenth Century*. Princeton: Princeton University Press.

Chiva, Isac. 1987. "Entre livre et musée: Emergence d'une ethnologie de la France." In Isac Chiva and Utz Jeggle, eds., *Ethnologies en miroir: La France et les pays de langue allemande*, 9–33. Paris: Editions de la maison des sciences de l'homme.

Chivallon, Christine. 2002. "Mémoires antillaises de l'esclavage." *Ethnologie française* 32, no. 4: 601–612.

Cole, Jeffrey. 1997. *The New Racism in Europe: A Sicilian Ethnography*. Cambridge: Cambridge University Press.

Conconne, Carine. 2003. "Un recul modéré du chômage." *Antiane-Eco* 57: 20–22.

Confiant, Raphaël. 1988. *Le nègre et l'amiral*. Paris: Grasset.

Constant, Fred. 1988. *La retraite aux flambeaux: Société et politique en Martinique*. Paris: Editions Caribéennes.

———. 1997. "La politique migratoire: Essai d'évaluation." In Fred Constant and Justin Daniel, eds., *1946–1996: Cinquante ans de départmentalisation outre-mer*, 97–132. Paris: L'Harmattan.

Constant, Fred, and Justin Daniel, eds. 1997. *1946–1996: Cinquante ans de départmentalisation outre-mer*. Paris: L'Harmattan.

Crusol, Jean. 1975. "Quelques aspects économiques de la départmentalisation aux Antilles françaises." *Révue économique du sud-ouest*. 24: 211–223.

Cuisenier, Jean. 1991. "Que faire des arts et traditions populaires?" *Le Débat* 65: 150–164.

Damas, Léon Gontran. 1972. *Pigments, névralgies*. Paris: Présence Africaine.

Daniel, Justin. 1997. Introduction to Fred Constant and Justin Daniel, eds., *1946–1996: Cinquante ans de départmentalisation outre-mer*, 11–22. Paris: L'Harmattan.

———. 2002. L'espace politique aux Antilles françaises. *Ethnologie française* 32, no. 4: 589–600.

Dominguez, Virginia. 1986. *White by Definition: Social Classification in Creole Louisiana*. New Brunswick, N.J.: Rutgers University Press.

Donzelot, Jacques. 1994. *L'invention du social*. Paris: Seuil.

Dorigny, Marcel, ed. 1999. *Escalvage, resistances et abolitions.* Paris: Editions du CTHS.

Dubet, François. 1987. *La galère: Jeunes en survie.* Paris: Fayard.

Dubois, Laurent. 1999. "'The Price of Liberty': Victor Hugues and the Administration of Freedom in Guadeloupe, 1794–1798." *William and Mary Quarterly* 56, no. 2: 363–392.

———. 2000. "La République Métissée: Citizenship, Colonialism, and the Borders of French History." *Cultural Studies* 14, no. 1: 15–34.

Durkheim, Emile. [1893] 1947. *The Division of Labor in Society.* Glencoe, Ill.: Free Press.

———. [1912] 1965. *The Elementary Forms of the Religious Life.* New York: Free Press.

Dumont, Louis. 1986. *Essays on Individualism: Modern Ideology in Anthropological Perspective.* Chicago: University of Chicago Press.

Espaces 89. 1985. *L'identité française.* Paris: Tierce.

Fanon, Frantz. 1952. *Peau noire masques blancs.* Paris: Seuil.

———. 1967. *Black Skin, White Masks.* Translated by Charles Lam Markmann. New York: Grove.

Favell, Adrian. 1997. "Citizenship and Immigration: Pathologies of a Progressive Philosophy." *New Community* 23, no. 2: 173–195.

Feldblum, Miriam. 1999. *Reconstructing Citizenship: The Politics of Nationality Reform and Immigration in Contemporary France.* Albany: SUNY Press.

Foucault, Michel. 1981. "Truth and Power." In Charles C. Lemert, ed., *French Sociology: Rupture and Renewal since 1968,* 293–307. New York: Columbia University Press.

François-Lubin, Bertrand. 1997. "Les méandres de la politique sociale outre mer." In Fred Constant and Justin Daniel, eds., *1946–1996: Cinquante ans de départmentalisation outre-mer,* 73–95. Paris: L'Harmattan.

Galap, Jean. 1987. "Dossier insertion sociale." *Mawon* 1: 13–104.

Ghasarian, Christian. 1994. "L'anthropologie américaine en son miroir." *L'Homme* 34, no. 3: 137–144.

Gilroy, Paul. 1993. *The Black Atlantic: Modernity and Double Consciousness.* Cambridge: Harvard University Press.

———. 1990. "One Nation Under a Groove: The Cultural Politics of 'Race' and Racism in Britain." In David Theo Goldberg, ed., *Anatomy of Racism,* 263–282. Minneapolis: University of Minnesota Press.

———. 1987. *"There Ain't No Black in the Union Jack": The Cultural Politics of Race and Nation.* Chicago: University of Chicago Press.

Giraud, Michel. 1979. *Races et classes à la Martinique.* Paris: Anthropos.

———. 1985. "Sommes-nous français?" In Jean-Yves Potel, ed., *L'etat de la France et de ses habitants.* Paris: Découverte.

———. 1997. "De la négritude à la créolité: Une évolution paradoxale à l'ère départementale." In Fred Constant and Justin Daniel, eds., *1946–1996: Cinquante ans de départmentalisation outre-mer,* 373–403. Paris: L'Harmattan.

———. 1999. "La patrimonialisation des cultures antillaises." *Ethnologie française* 29, no. 3: 375–386.

Giraud, Michel and Jean-Luc Jamard. 1982. Contre l'économisme: le cas antillais. *Critiques de L'Economie Politique.* 20:110-142.

Glissant, Edouard. 1981. *Le discours antillais.* Paris: Seuil.

_____. 1989. *Caribbean Discourse: Selected Essays.* Translated and edited by J. Michael Dash. Charlottesville: University Press of Virginia.

Greenhouse, Carol J., and Davydd J. Greenwood. 1998. "Introduction: The Ethnography of Democracy and Difference." In Carol J. Greenhouse, ed., *Democracy and Ethnography: Constructing Identities in Multicultural Liberal States,* 1–24. Albany: SUNY Press.

Gregory, Steven. 1998. *Black Corona: Race and the Politics of Place in an Urban Community.* Princeton: Princeton University Press.

Grillo, R. D. 1985. *Ideologies and Institutions in Urban France: The Representation of Immigrants.* Cambridge: Cambridge University Press.

Guillaumin, Colette. 1981. "'Je sais bien mais quand même' ou les avatars de la notion 'race.'" In *Le genre humain 1. La science face au racisme,* 55–65. Paris: Fayard.

Hall, Kathleen. 2002. *Lives in Translation: Sikh Youth as British Citizens.* Philadelphia: University of Pennsylvania Press.

Handler, Richard. 1988. *Nationalism and the Politics of Culture in Quebec.* Madison: University of Wisconsin Press.

Hargreaves, Alec G. 1995. *Immigration, "Race," and Ethnicity in Contemporary France.* London: Routledge.

_____. 1996. "A Deviant Construction: The French Media and the 'Banlieues.'" *New Community* 22, no. 4: 607–618.

Hargreaves, Alec G., and Mark McKinney. 1997. "The Post-Colonial Problematic in Contemporary France." In Alec G. Hargreaves and Mark McKinney, eds., *Post-Colonial Cultures in France,* 3–25. London: Routledge.

Hazareesingh, Sudhir. 1994. *Political Traditions in Modern France.* Oxford: Oxford University Press.

Hélias, Pierre-Jakez. 1978. *The Horse of Pride: Life in a Breton Village.* New Haven: Yale University Press.

Herzfeld, Michael. 1987. *Anthropology Through the Looking-Glass: Critical Ethnography in the Margins of Europe.* Cambridge: Cambridge University Press.

_____. 1992. *The Social Production of Indifference: Exploring the Symbolic Roots of Western Bureaucracy.* Chicago: University of Chicago Press.

Horne, Janet R. 2002. *A Social Laboratory for Modern France. The Musée Social and the Rise of the Welfare State.* Durham, N.C.: Duke University Press.

Horowitz, Michael M. 1967. *Morne Paysan: Peasant Village in Martinique.* New York: Holt, Rinehart & Winston.

Hyatt, Susan Brin. 1997. "Poverty in a 'Post-Welfare' Landscape: Tenant Management Policies, Self-Governance and the Democratization of Knowledge in Great Britain." In Cris Shore and Susan Wright, eds., *Anthropology of Policy: Critical Perspectives on Governance and Power,* 217–238. New York: Routledge.

Ireland, Patrick. 1994. *The Policy Challenge of Ethnic Diversity: Immigrant Politics in France and Switzerland*. Cambridge: Harvard University Press.

Jardel, Jean-Pierre. 1978. "Français et créole dans le conflit interculturel à la Martinique." In A. Valdman, ed., *Le français hors de France*, 145–163. Paris: Editions Champion.

Jennings, Lawrence. 2000. *French Anti-Slavery: The Movement for the Abolition of Slavery in France, 1802–1848*. Cambridge: Cambridge University Press.

Kadish, Doris, ed. 2000. *Slavery in the Caribbean Francophone World: Distant Voices, Forgotten Acts, Forged Identities*. Athens: University of Georgia Press.

Kaplan, Steven. 1995. *Farewell, Revolution: Disputed Legacies, France, 1789/1989*. Ithaca: Cornell University Press.

Kauppi, Niilo. 1996. *French Intellectual Nobility: Institutional and Symbolic Transformations in the Post-Sartrian Era*. Albany: State University of New York Press.

Kennedy, Ellen Conroy. 1975. *The Negritude Poets: An Anthology of Translations from the French*. New York: Thunder's Mouth.

Kepel, Gilles. 1987. *Les banlieues de l'Islam*. Paris: Seuil.

Khan, Aisha. 2001. "Journey to the Center of the Earth: The Caribbean as Master Symbol." *Cultural Anthropology* 16, no. 3: 271–302.

Lacroix, Pierre. 1989. "Migration antillaise, guadeloupéens et martiniquais en France: Repères pour un service pastoral." *Cahiers de la pastorales des migrants* 18–19.

Lebovics, Herman. 1992. *True France: The Wars over Cultural Identity, 1900–1945*. Ithaca: Cornell University Press.

Lehmann, Richard. 1987. *Les adventistes du septième jour*. Paris: Brepols.

Lehning, James R. 1995. *Peasant and French: Culture Contact in Rural France During the Nineteenth Century*. Cambridge: Cambridge University Press.

Leiris, Michel. 1955. *Contacts de civilisations en Martinique et en Guadeloupe*. Paris: UNESCO/Gallimard.

Leruth, Michael F. 1998a. "François Mitterrand's 'Festival of the World's Tribes': The Logic of Exoticism in the French Revolution bicentennial Parade." *French Cultural Studies* 9: 51–80.

_____. 1998b. "The Neorepublican Discourse on French National Identity." *French Politics and Society* 16, no. 4: 46–61.

Lévi-Strauss, Claude. 1973. *Tristes tropiques*. New York: Atheneum.

Limón, José. 1999. *American Encounters: Greater Mexico, the United States, and the Erotics of Culture*. Boston: Beacon.

Lirus, Julie. 1979. *Identité antillaise*. Paris: Editions Caribéennes.

Marie, Claude-Valentin. 1993a. "Les populations des DOM-TOM, nées et originaires, résidant en France métropolitaine, résultats du sondage au quart. *INSEE résultats* 232.

_____. 1993b. "Histoire et réalités d'une immigration ambiguë." *Alizés* 43, no. 1: 7–11.

_____. 2002. "Les antillais en France: Une nouvelle donne." *Hommes et migrations* 1237: 26–39.

Markovits, Andrei. 1998. "Reflections on the World Cup '98." *French Politics and Society* 16, no. 3: 1–29.

Martinez-Alier, Verena. 1989. *Marriage, Class, and Color in Nineteenth Century Cuba.* Ann Arbor: University of Michigan Press.

Massé, Raymond. 1978. *Les adventistes du septième jour aux Antilles françaises.* Fonds St. Jacques, Martinique: Centre de recherche caraïbes.

Mauss, Marcel. [1954] 1969. *Oeuvres 3. Cohésion sociale et divisions de la sociologie.* Paris: Editions de Minuit.

Migerel, Helène. 1987. *La migration des zombis: Survivances de la magie antillaise en France.* Paris: Editions Caribéennes.

_____. 1989. "Rôle et place de la magie dans l'éducation." *Mawon* 3: 69–77.

Miles, William F. S. 1986. *Elections and Ethnicity in French Martinique: A Paradox in Paradise.* New York: Praeger.

_____. 1999. "Abolition, Independence, and Soccer: Premillennial Dilemmas of Martinican Identity." *French Politics and Society* 17, no. 2: 23–33.

Mosse, George L. 1978. *Toward the Final Solution: A History of European Racism.* Madison: University of Wisconsin Press.

Murray, David A. B. 1997. "The Cultural Citizen: Negations of Race and Language in the Making of Martiniquais." *Anthropological Quarterly* 70, no. 2: 79–90.

_____. 2002. *Opacity: Gender, Sexuality, Race, and the "Problem" of Identity in Martinique.* New York: Peter Lang.

Noiriel, Gérard. 1988. *Le creuset français: Histoire de l'immigration, XIXe–XXe siècles.* Paris: Seuil.

_____. 1996. *The French Melting Pot: Immigration, Citizenship, and National Identity.* Translated by Geoffroy de Laforcade. Minneapolis: University of Minnesota Press.

Northcutt, Wayne. 1991. "François Mitterrand and the Political Use of Symbols: The Construction of a Centrist Republic." *French Historical Studies* 17, no. 1: 141–158.

Nosel, José. 1997. "Appréciation de l'impact économique de la departmentalisation à la Martinique." In Fred Constant and Justin Daniel, eds., *1946–1996: Cinquante ans de départmentalisation outre-mer,* 25–71. Paris: L'Harmattan.

Omi, Michael, and Howard Winant. 1986. *Racial Formation in the United States.* New York: Routledge.

Ong, Aihwa. 1999. *Flexible Citizenship: The Cultural Logics of Transnationality.* Durham, N.C.: Duke University Press.

Panoff, Michel. 1986. "Une valeur sûre: L'exotisme." In *Revue l'homme, anthropologie: Etat des lieux,* 321–331. Paris: Navarin.

Pastel, Pierre. 1987. "Regards sur la vie associative des antillais et guyanais en France." *Alizés,* 3–11.

Pellissier, Jérôme, ed. 2001. *A but non lucrative: 1901–2001, cent ans de liberté d'association.* Paris: Editions Fischbacher.

Price, Richard. 1998. *The Convict and the Colonel*. Boston: Beacon.

———. 2001a. "The Miracle of Creolization: A Retrospective." *New West Indian Guide* 75, no. 1–2: 35–64.

———. 2001b. "'Monuments and Silent Screamings': A View from Martinique." In G. Oostindie, *Facing up to the Past: Perspectives on the Commemoration of Slavery from Africa, the Americas, and Europe*, 58–62. Kingston: Ian Randle.

Price, Richard, and Sally Price. 1997. "Shadowboxing in the Mangrove." *Cultural Anthropology* 12, no. 1: 3–36.

Prost, Antoine. 1968. *Histoire de l'enseignement en France*. Paris: Colin.

Prudent, Lambert-Félix. 1983. "La langue créole aux Antilles et en Guyane." *Les temps modernes* 441–442: 2072–2089.

———. 1993. "Political Illusions of an Intervention in the Linguistic Domain in Martinique." *International Journal of the Sociology of Language* 102: 135–148.

Ragi, Tariq. 1998. *Acteurs de l'intégration: Les associations et les pratiques éducatives*. Paris: L'Harmattan.

Renan, Ernest. [1882] 1992. *Qu'est-ce qu'une nation? et autres essais politiques*. Paris: Presses Pocket.

Réno, Fred. 1997. "La créolisation de l'espace public à la Martinique." In Fred Constant and Justin Daniel, eds., *1946–1996: Cinquante ans de départmentalisation outre-mer*, 405–431. Paris: L'Harmattan.

Rogers, Susan Carol. 1987. "Good to Think: The 'Peasant' in Contemporary France." *Anthropological Quarterly* 60: 56–63.

———. 1991. *Shaping Modern Times in Rural France*. Princeton: Princeton University Press.

———. 2001. "Anthropology in France." *Annual Review of Anthropology* 30: 481–504.

Rosello, Mirelle. 1998. "Representing Illegal Immigrants in France: From Clandestins to L'affaire Des Sans Papiers de Saint-Bernard." *Journal of European Studies* 28, no. 1–2: 137–152.

Sanjek, Roger. 1998. *The Future of Us All: Race and Neighborhood Politics in New York City*. Ithaca: Cornell University Press.

Satineau, Maurice. 1986. *Contestation politique et revendication nationaliste aux Antilles françaises dans un contexte électoral*. Paris: L'Harmattan.

Segal, Daniel. 1993. "'Race' and 'Colour' in Pre-Independence Trinidad and Tobago." In Kevin A. Yelvington, ed., *Trinidad Ethnicity*. Knoxville: University of Tennessee Press.

Sartre, Jean-Paul. 1954. *Réflexions sur la question juive*. Paris: Gallimard.

Schiller, Nina Glick, and Georges Fouron. 2001. *Georges Woke Up Laughing: Long-Distance Nationalism and the Search for Home*. Durham, N.C.: Duke University Press.

Schmidt, Nelly. 1999. "Commémoration, histoire et historiographie: A propos du 150e anniversaire de l'abolition de l'esclavage dans les colonies françaises." *Ethnologie française* 29, no. 3: 453–460.

Schneider, William. 1990. *Quality and Quantity: The Quest for Biological Regeneration in Twentieth-Century France.* New York: Cambridge University Press.

———. 1994. "Hérédité, sang et opposition à l'immigration dans la France des années trente." *Ethnologie française* 24: 104–117.

Schnepel, Ellen M. 1993. "The Creole Movement in Guadeloupe." *International Journal for the Sociology of Language* 102: 117–134.

Silverstein, Paul A. 2000. "Sporting Faith: Islam, Soccer, and the French Nation-State." *Social Text* 18, no. 4: 25–53.

Stolcke, Verena. 1995. "Talking Culture: New Boundaries, New Rhetorics of Exclusion in Europe." *Current Anthropology* 36, no. 1: 1–24.

Stovall, Tyler, and Georges Van Den Abbeele, eds. 2003. *French Civilization and Its Discontents: Nationalism, Colonialism, Race.* Lanham, Md.: Lexington.

Suvélor, Roland. 1983. "Eléments historiques pour une approche socio-culturelle." *Temps modernes* 441–442: 2174–2208.

Taguieff, Pierre-André. 1994. "Eugénisme ou décadence? L'exception française." *Ethnologie française* 24: 81–103.

Templeton, Alan R. 1999. "Human Races: A Genetic and Evolutionary Perspective." *American Anthropologist* 100, no. 3: 632–650.

Terrio, Susan J. 1999. "Crucible of the Millennium?: The Clovis Affair in Contemporary France." *Comparative Studies in Society and History* 41: 438–457.

Todorov, Tzvetan. 1989. *Nous et les autres: La réflexion française sur la diversité humaine.* Paris: Seuil.

Torgovnick, Marianna. 1990. *Gone Primitive: Savage Intellects, Modern Lives.* Chicago: University of Chicago Press.

Toulis, Nicole Rodriguez. 1997. *Believing Identity: Pentecostalism and the Mediation of Jamaican Ethnicity and Gender in England.* Oxford: Berg.

Ullman, Claire F. 1998. *The Welfare State's Other Crisis: Explaining the New Partnership Between Nonprofit Organizations and the State in France.* Bloomington: Indiana University Press.

Van Beek, Martijn. 2000. "Beyond Identity Fetishism: 'Communal' Conflict in Ladakh and the Limits of Autonomy." *Cultural Anthropology* 15, no. 4: 525–569.

Vergès, Françoise. 1999. *Monsters and Revolutionaries: Colonial Family Romance and Métissage.* Durham, N.C.: Duke University Press.

Wacquant, Loïc. 1993. "Urban Outcasts: Stigma and Division in the Black American Ghetto and the French Urban Periphery." *International Journal of Urban and Regional Research* 17, no. 3: 366–383.

Weber, Eugen. 1976. *Peasants into Frenchmen.* Stanford: Stanford University Press.

Werbner, Pnina. 2002. *Imagined Diasporas Among Manchester Muslims: The Public Performance of Pakistani Transnational Identity Politics.* Santa Fe: School of American Research Press.

Werbner, Pnina, and Tariq Modood, eds. 1997. *Debating Cultural Hybridity: Multi-Cultural Identities and the Politics of Anti-Racism.* London: Zed.

Weil, Patrick, and John Crowley. 1994. "Integration in Theory and Practice: A Comparison of France and Britain." *West European Politics* 17, no. 2: 110–126.

Wieviorka, Michel. 1997. "Culture, société et démocratie." In Michel Wieviorka, ed., *Une société fragmentée? Le multiculturalisme en débat.* Paris: La Découverte.

Wihtol de Wenden, Catherine. 1988. *Les immigrés et la politique.* Paris: Presses de la Fondation Nationale des Sciences Politiques.

_____. 1991. "North African Immigration and the French Political Imaginary." In Maxim Silverman, ed., *Race, Discourse, and Power in France,* 98–110. Aldershot, U.K.: Avebury.

Wihtol de Wenden, Catherine, and Rémy Leveau. 2001. *La bourgeoisie: Les trois ages de la vie associative issue de l'immigration.* Paris: CNRS Editions.

Williams, Raymond. 1977. *Marxism and Literature.* Oxford: Oxford University Press.

Winock, Michel. 1990. *Nationalisme, antisémitisme et fascisme en France.* Paris: Seuil.

Yelvington, Kevin A. 1995. *Producing Power: Ethnicity, Gender, and Class in a Caribbean Workplace.* Philadelphia: Temple University Press.

_____. 2001. "The Anthropology of Afro-Latin America and the Caribbean: Diasporic Dimensions." *Annual Review of Anthropology* 30: 227–260.

Zobel, Joseph. 1974. *La Rue Cases-Nègres.* Paris: Présence Africaine.

Index

Abu-Lughod, Lila, 21n3
Action Catholique, 108
Adieu Foulards, 82, 83
Agence Nationale pour l'Insertion et la Promotion des Travailleurs d'Outre-Mer (ANT), 16, 65, 66, 76, 78, 93, 97
Alizés, 112
All Saints Day, 110
Anticlericalism, 112
Anti–89, 80
Antillanité, 11, 14, 67–71, 72
Antillean community, 18, 20
Antillean Catholic activism, 105–107, 109–113
    lay leadership, 109
    lay organizing, 112, 113
Antillean population in France, 21n1, 63, 64
    as "third island", 61, 129
    as cultural outsiders, xvi, xviii, 7, 20–21, 47, 64, 70, 80, 128
    as foreigners, 63
    before 1960s, 64
    characteristics, 64
    second generation, 64, 85, 86
Antillean religious practices, 112. *See also* Catholic Church; Catholicism; Religion; Seventh-Day Adventists
Anti-Semitism, 34
Appadurai, Arjun, 21n1
Assimilation, xvi-xix, 7, 10, 14, 18, 37, 63, 66, 103, 125, 127–130, 132
    antillanité as critique, 68
    anticolonialist ideology, 57, 59, 61, 128
    créolité as critique, 70–71
    education, 57
    gender, 80
    négritude as critique, 67
    non-profit associations, 77
    Seventh-Day Adventist Church, 116
Augé, Marc, 48n15
Aumônerie Catholique Antilles-Guyane de Paris, 16, 105, 111, 112
    ethnic mission, 109, 111
Aznavour, Charles, 30

Balibar, Etienne, 42
Bambuck, Roger, 102
Bangou, Henri, 27–29
Barrès, Maurice, 35, 126
Bastien, Daniel, 72n12
Bastille Day, 25–27, 33
Baumann, Gerd, 21n3, 22n12, 22
Beauharnais, Joséphine de, 1, 3, 83
Beausire, Bruno, 88n3
van Beek, Martijn, 21n3
Békés, 4, 57, 60, 74, 128
Bélè, 14
Bernabé, Jean, 12, 13, 68, 72
Bête humaine, la, 26
Beur, 45
Bicentennial of the French revolution,
    xvii, xviii, 25–27, 32, 33, 42, 47, 51,
    75, 80, 133
    Antillean reactions, 27–29, 85
Birnbaum, Pierre, 35, 49
Black Atlantic, xvii, xx
Black Skin, White Masks (Fanon), xvi
Boëldieu, Julien, 21n1
Bonaparte, Napoleon, 28, 52, 83
Bongie, Chris, 71n3
Borrel, Catherine, 21n1
Boudin, 80
Breton, André, 62
Brodwin, Paul, 121
Browne, Katherine, 22n4, 22n7
Brown, Jacqueline Nassy, 22n12
Brubaker, Rogers, 49
Bureau pour les Migrations Intéressant
    les Départements d'Outre-mer
    (BUMIDOM), 64, 65
Burton, Richard D. E., 72

Cabo, Ernest, 105, 106
Cahier d'un retour au pays natal, 67
Calalou de crabe, 3
Canon des nègre marrons, 83, 84
Caribbean diaspora, xiii, 68, 81
Carnival, 13, 56

Carter, Donald Martin, 121
Catholic Church, 27, 33, 37, 105–113
    center for Antillean community,
        107, 113
    compared to Seventh-Day Adventists,
        111, 119–120
    creolization, 131
    ethnic organizing, 110
    in contemporary France, 109, 111
    Portuguese immigrant community,
        110
    resistance to Second Vatican Council
        in France, 80
    social activism, 93, 108, 131
Catholicism, xv, xix, xx, 6, 35, 126
    forced conversion of African
        slaves, 94
    in Martinique and Guadeloupe, 111
    relationship to Antillean magic, 95
Centre d'Entraide et d'Etude des
    Antillais, Guyanais, Réunionnais
    (CEDAGR), 89–103, 111, 112, 123,
    124, 131, 132
Centrale Syndicale des Travailleurs
    Martiniquais (CSTM), 13, 20
Césaire, Aimé, xvii, xix, 10, 14, 67, 68,
    69, 72
    Cahier d'un retour au pays natal,
        67, 72
Chamoiseau, Patrick, xix, 10, 13, 22n5,
    68–70, 72
Chenière, Ernest, 31, 128
Chirac, Jacques, 47, 52, 125
Chivallon, Christine, 71n3
Citizenship, 37, 59
    making French citizens, 76
Closed nationalism, 35, 36, 47, 126
Clovis, 43
Cole, Jeffrey, 49
Colombo de porc, 80
Colonialism, xiii, xvi, xix, 54, 62, 67,
    69, 91
Colonial ideology, 102

Comment faire l'amour avec un nègre sans se fatiguer, 39, 40
Concrete intellectuals, 94
Condé, Maryse, 10
Confédération française de travailleurs chrétiens (CFTC), 108
Confiant, Raphaël, 10, 13, 68–70, 72n11, 72, 83
Conseil Général, 59
Conseil Régional, 59
Corsicans, 4, 6, 98
Cosby, Bill, 38
    Cosby Show, 38, 39
Coulis, 57
Creil, 31
Creole hymns, 106, 107, 119
Creole identity, 18–20
Creole language, xiv, 12–14, 20, 69, 74, 77, 124
    CAPES de créole, 125
    Creole curriculum, 12, 125
    International Creole Day, 123–125
    magic, 95
    performances in, 83
    regional language policy, 125
    Seventh-Day Adventist Church, 115, 116
    suppression in schools, 57
    teaching degree, 125
Créolité, xvii, xix, 13, 14, 20, 22n9, 68–72
    appeal to Antilleans in France, 70, 129
    as food, 62
    International Creole Day, 124
Creolization, xvii, xix, xx, 13, 22n9, 131, 132, 133
Crowley, John, 22n13
Crusol, Jean, 72n12
Cultural fundamentalism, 37, 42, 77, 81. *See also* Republican fundamentalism
Cultural heritage
    French, 36

Culture, 7–8, 33–36. *See also Culture*
    commodity, 14
    concept in anthropology, 21n3
    cultural citizenship, 14, 75
    cultural hinterland, 66
    cultural policy, 75, 76
    cultural recognition, 6, 7, 66, 92, 98, 128
    fetish, 76
    folk culture, 63, 68, 76, 83, 126, 133
    Ministry of Culture, 75, 76, 77
    regional culture, 76, 126
    universal, 76
Culture, 8, 75, 77, 83, 130. *See also* Culture
    Antillean, 14, 68, 75, 84, 85, 86, 129, 130
    as race, 36–42
    between two cultures, 92, 126
    black, 67
    Caribbean, 81, 87
    creolized, 81, 124
    cultures, 124
    deculturation, 96
    European, 67
    French, 33–36, 68, 75, 76, 86, 125, 126
    globalized, 76, 88
    high *culture*, 75, 76, 86, 87
    immigrant, 77
    négritude and, 67
    stereotypes, 84, 87
Culturel, le, 7, 75, 77, 131
    and public policy, 93, 103
Culture shock, 8, 10

Damas, Léon Gontron, 22n14, 67, 69
    Hiccups, 82, 83
Damier, 83, 86
Declaration of the Rights of Man and of the Citizen, 25, 28
    slavery and, 28
De Gaulle, Charles, 85
Delgrès, Louis, 29, 53

Departmentalization, xix, 60, 128
   political demand in Antilles, 59, 67
Départements d'outre-mer. See Overseas
   departments
Désir, Harlem, 5, 85
Dezormo, Djo, 13
Doc Gynéco, 88n3
Dominguez, Virginia, 22n11
Do the Right Thing, 86
Dorigny, Marcel, 48n6
Dreyfus, Alfred, 52
Dubois, Laurent, 47n1, 48n6, 48n8
Dumont, Louis, 41
Durkheim, Emile, 34, 37, 39, 41
   Division of Labor in Society, 34
   *Elementary Forms of the Religious
      Life*, 41

Eboué, Félix, 53
Ecole des Hautes Etudes en Sciences
   Sociales, 51
Edict of Nantes, 52
Education
   ethnic communities, 31
   religious communities, 31
   secular, 33
Eloge, 16, 73–75, 77–81, 87, 123
   experiences of racism, 80, 81, 130
   1901 law association, 78
   rejection of assimilation, 130
Eloge de la créolité, 68, 70, 72, 133
Ethnic activism, 5
   in Catholic Church, 110
Ethnic communities in France, 33, 125,
   126, 133
Ethnic ghettos, 92
Ethnicity, xvii, 17, 18, 90
   primordial, 21
   tribalism, 31
Ethnicization of crime and poverty,
   42–43, 46–47, 127, 131
Ethnic voting blocs, 73
Ethnography, xvii

Et le sang gicla, 74
Etudiant noir, L', 67
European Charter for Regional or
   Minority Languages, 125
European market, 29
European Union, xix, 13, 100, 133
Exclusif, 55

Fanon, Frantz, xvi, xvii, xix, 10, 67,
   72n11
   Black Skin, White Masks, xvi, 72
Favell, Adrian, 22n13
Feldblum, Miriam, 49
Festival Caraibe, 68
Field research, xiv, xviii, 1
   postmodern, 20
Finkielkraut, Alain, 34, 46
Folklore, 35, 126, 130
Fonds d'action et de soutien pour
   l'intégration et la lutte contre les
   discriminations (FASILD), 103n1
Fonds d'action sociale pour les
   travailleurs immigrés et leurs
   familles(FAS), 76, 92, 93, 97, 103n1
Foulards islamiques, 31–33, 43, 125, 128,
   132
   Conseil d'Etat ruling, 31, 32
Fouron, Georges, 134
Freedom of religion, 107
Free men of color, 28, 55
French Antilles
   colonies, 61
   economy, 60–61
   immigration to, 61
   political equality, 59–60, 128
   representation in French National
      Assembly, 59
French national culture, 33–36, 76
French Revolution, 25–28

Gabin, Jean, 26, 30
Galap, Jean, 16, 89, 90, 93, 94, 97, 99,
   100, 102, 103, 112

Galère, la, 103
Gilroy, Paul, xvii, 48n18, 88
Giraud, Michel, 6, 72n12
Glissant, Edouard, xix, 10, 11, 66–70, 72
Grands blancs, 55
Greenhouse, Carol J., 21n3
Greenwood, Davydd J., 21n3
Grégoire, Abbé, 53
Groupe de recherches et d'études en
    espace créole (GEREC), 124,
    134n1
Groupe de recherches et d'études en
    espace créole et francophone
    (GEREC-F), 134n1
Group of Seven Leading Industrialized
    Nations, 25
Guadeloupe
  geography, 54
  history, 27–29, 54–61
Guadeloupe Solidarité, 99–102
Guigou, Elisabeth, 53
Guillaumin, Colette, 48n18
Gwoka, 14

Hall, Kathleen, 21n3, 22
Handler, Richard, 21n3
Hargreaves, Alec G., 22n13, 49, 88
Hate, 43
Hélias, Pierre-Jakez, 72n11
Herzfeld, Michael, 21n3
Hip-hop, 88, 88n3
Housing discrimination, 90
Human rights, 25, 26, 51
  Universal Declaration of Human
      Rights, 52
Hurricane Hugo, 98–102, 106
Hyatt, Susan Brin, 103

Immigration
  Antilleans in France, characteristics,
      64
  community reflex, 32, 126
  European Union, 30

history in France, 29, 30
  illegal, 43
  immigrant activism, 7, 10
  immigrant population, 30
  immigrant problem, 3, 7, 21, 70
  immigrant rights coalitions, 5
  immigrés, 30, 126
  insecurity, 47
  North African, 126
  Pre World War II, 30
  post World War II, 36, 125
  racialization, 30, 103
  second generation, 88, 126
  secularism, 107
  social disorder, 42, 43, 127
  social policy, 92, 93
  sports, 46
  supportive cultural policy, 91
  Third World origins, 30, 33, 76, 125
  travailleurs étrangers, 30
Independentists, 13, 20
Integration, 42, 63, 102, 127
  American model, 43
  French model, 52
  policy, xiv, 46
Intercultural relations seminars, 89–91,
    97
International Creole Day, 123–125,
    133
Ireland, Patrick, 104
Islam, 43, 126
Islamic scarves. *See Foulards islamiques*

Jamard, Jean-Luc, 72n12
Jehovah's Witnesses, 109
Jeunesses Ouvrières Chrétiennes (JOC),
    108
Jews in France, 34
Jospin, Lionel, 31, 32, 52
July, Serge, 48n15

Kadish, Doris, 48n6
Kanaks, 41, 98

Kaplan, Steven, 47n1, 48n5
Kardec, Alain, 95
Kassovitz, Mathieu, 43
Khan, Aisha, 22n9

Labouré, Catherine, 95
Lacroix, Pierre, 16, 109–113
Lang, Jack, 125
Larifla, Dominique, 102
Latitudes, 41
Lee, Spike, 86
Légitime défense, 67
Leiris, Michel, 62
Le Pen, Jean-Marie, 35, 46, 47, 127
Le Pensec, Louis, 100, 101
Lévi-Strauss, Claude, 62
Lirus, Julie, 103n2
Lourdes, 110
Louverture, Toussaint, 29, 53, 83

Madras cloth, 74
Magic, 94–96
    Antillean, origins, 94
    civilization, 96
    guilt, 95
    landscape in Antilles, 95
    landscape in Paris, 95
    marker of cultural difference, 94
    mental illness, 96
    relationship to Catholicism, 95
    saints, 95
Makeba, Miriam, 41
Marie, Claude-Valentin, 21n1
Marrons, 55
Martinique
    "big box" French retail, 13
    geography, 54
    history, 54–61
    tourism, 13
    unemployment, 10, 13, 22n7
Mauss, Marcel, 34
Mawon, 94
McKinney, Mark, 22n13, 88

Mechanical solidarity, 39
Metacultural ideology, 90
Métèque, 89
Métissage, 91
Métropole, 14, 57, 59, 60, 97
Metros, 57
Migerel, Hélène, 94–96, 101, 103n2
Migration, transnational, xvii
Miles, William F.S., 71n3, 72n12
Ministry for Overseas Departments and
    Territories, 60, 97, 100
Mitterrand, François, 25, 27
Mobutu, President, 41
Modernity, 25, 26
Modood, Tariq, 134
Monnerville, Gaston, 85
Montand, Yves, 30
Morin, Edgar, 46
Multiculturalism, 20, 36, 46, 47, 76,
    88, 133
Murray, David A.B., 22n8, 88
Musée National des Arts et Traditions
    Populaires (ATP), 35, 76

National Front, 16, 35, 46
Nèg congo, 57
Négritude, xvii, xix, 14, 67–71
Neorepublican discourse, 18, 22n13.
    See also Cultural fundamentalism;
    Republican fundamentalism
New Caledonia, 41
1901 law associations, 65.
    See also Nonprofit associations
    immigrant leadership and
    organization, 65, 76, 92
Noiriel, Gérard, 34, 49
Noir, 16
Nonprofit associations, 65, 66, 129.
    See also 1901 law associations
    social policy, 93
    welfare state, 131
Norman, Jessye, 26, 42
Northcutt, Wayne, 47n1

Omi, Michael, 22n11
Organic solidarity, 34, 40
Overseas departments, xvi, 10, 22, 41, 59, 128
    natural disasters, 98

Panoff, Michel, 41
Pantheon, 27, 53
Pasqua, Charles, 46
Patrimoine culturel, 36, 76, 81, 86, 87, 124, 130
    journées du patrimoine, 36
Petits blancs, 55
Piment, xiv, 3
Pinalie, Pierre, 68
Popular Front, 35
Postcolonial, xv, xvi, xix, 7, 18, 62
    postcolonial domination, 10
    postcolonial France, xvii, 14
    postcolonials, xviii
Price, Richard, xvi, 14, 22n9, 23, 71n3, 88
Price, Sally, 22n9, 88
Prudent, Lambert-Félix, 12

Queyranne, Jean-Jacques, 53

Race, xvi, xvii, 7, 16, 17, 33, 34
    color, 37
    culture as, 36–42, 126, 127
    in France, 34, 126
    in Martinique and Guadeloupe, 55–57
    race relations, 6, 39
    scientific perspectives, 22n11
Racial determinism, 34
Racial ideologies, 37
Racialization, xix, xx, 103
Racism, xiii, xvi, xix, xx, 4, 5, 6, 16–18, 37–42, 53, 63, 74, 129, 132
    and cultural identity, 85
    housing discrimination, 90
    imperialist, 76
    religion, 106, 108

scientific, 37
Seventh-Day Adventist Church, 118
    without races, 6, 127
Radio Beur, 101
Regicide, 80
Regional languages, 125
Religion, 105–121, 131. See also
    Catholic Church; Catholicism;
    Seventh-Day Adventists
    and magic, 94
    Antillean practices, 112
    Ministry of the Interior, 107
    religious communities, 31
    religious symbols in schools, 31
    representative organizations, 107
Renan, Ernest, 6, 34
Réno, Fred, 22n9, 72
Republican fundamentalism, 103, 125, 127, 131, 132, See also Cultural fundamentalism
Republican universalism, 34, 42, 125, 126
Rogers, Susan Carol, 22n6
Rotary Club, xiv, 1, 6
Rue du Bac, 95

Sans papiers, 43, 46, 127
Sartre, Jean-Paul, 7, 36
Schiller, Nina Glick, 134
Schmidt, Nelly, 71n3
Schoelcher, Victor, 27, 52, 53
Schwartz-Bart, Simone, 10
Secularism in France, 107, 108, 132
Senghor, Léopold, 67, 69
Separation of Church and State, 107.
    See also Religion
Service Municipal d'Action Culturelle (SERMAC), 11, 22n8
Seventh-Day Adventists, xx, 109, 113–120, 131–132. See also
    Catholic Church; Catholicism;
    Religion
    Antillean church, 116
    churches in Paris, 113

Service Municipal d'Action Culturelle
(SERMAC) *(continued)*
compared with Catholic Church, 111,
119–120
eschatology, 114
French Adventist Federation, 118, 119
French assimilationist ideology, 116
lifestyle, 117
paradox, 116, 117
politics, 116
racism, 118, 119
Sabbath school, 114
separatist church, 119
spiritual Israel, 114
warmth, 118
white church, 118
Shrub, xiv
Slavery, 1, 29, 55, 91, 128
abolition, xviii, 28, 51–54
bicentennial of 1794 abolition, 53
crime against humanity, 52, 54
French revolution, 27
150th anniversary of abolition,
51–54, 70, 102, 133
reestablishment, 28, 53
slave uprisings, 28
Social exclusion, 46, 103, 127, 131
poverty, 103, 127
Social insertion, xv, 93
Social, le, 7, 91, 93, 131
Social solidarity, 91
Société des Amis des Noirs, 28.
See also Slavery
SOS Racisme, 5, 85
South Africa, 41
Stade de France, 44. *See also* World Cup
of Soccer
Stand-Fast, 81–88, 130
Creolizing French culture, 131
tchimbé rèd, 81
St. Denis, 44, 46, 68, 105, 106, 109
Stolcke, Verena, 21n3
Stovall, Tyler, 23

St. Pierre and Miquelon, 41
Syro-Libanais, 57

Templeton, Alan R., 22n11
Terrorism, 43
Third World, xvii, 125
Threshold of tolerance, 42, 92, 118, 127.
See also Racism
Thuram, Lilian, 45
Ti'punch, 9
Toulis, Nicole Rodriguez, 121
Trautmann, Catherine, 51, 52
Triangular trade, 28, 48n7
True France, 35, 126

Ullman, Claire, 104
Unchain Your Citizenship, 52

Van Den Abbeele, George, 23
Vergès, Françoise, 134
Vodou, 94

Wacquant, Loïc, 22n12
Wallis and Futuna, 41
Weil, Patrick, 22n13
Welfare state, 91, 103, 128, 131
Werbner, Pnina, 121, 134
Wieviorka, Michel, 22n13
Winant, Howard, 22n11
Worker priests, 108
World Cup of Soccer, xvii, xviii, 42,
43–46, 102, 127, 133

Xenophobia. *See* Racism

Yelvington, Kevin A., 22n9

Zaire, 41
Zidane, Zinedine, 45, 46
Zobel, Joseph, 10, 72n11
Zola, Emile, 52
Z'oreilles, 57
Zouk, xvi, 16, 80, 81, 102, 116

For Product Safety Concerns and Information please contact our EU
representative GPSR@taylorandfrancis.com
Taylor & Francis Verlag GmbH, Kaufingerstraße 24, 80331 München, Germany

www.ingramcontent.com/pod-product-compliance
Ingram Content Group UK Ltd.
Pitfield, Milton Keynes, MK11 3LW, UK
UKHW010813080625
459435UK00006B/65